REAL CHANGE
IS INCREMENTAL

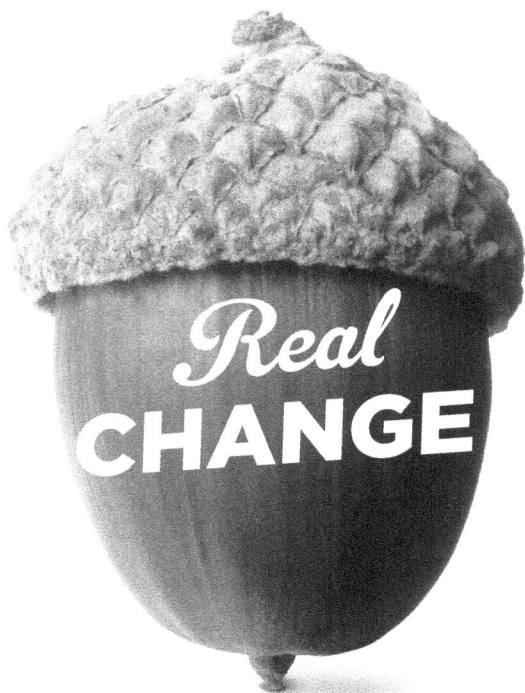

Real
CHANGE

IS

INCREMENTAL

REFLECTIONS ON WHAT WE KNOW, WHAT WE DO
AND HOW LITTLE THINGS MAKE A BIG DIFFERENCE

DAVID PECK

FOREWORD BY RUPEN DAS

BPS
books

Published in 2014 by
BPS Books
Toronto and New York
www.bpsbooks.com
A division of Bastian Publishing Services Ltd.

ISBN 978-1-927483-86-2 (paperback)
ISBN 978-1-927483-87-9 (ePDF)
ISBN 978-1-927483-88-6 (ePUB)

Cataloguing-in-Publication Data available from Library and Archives Canada.

Standing on the Edge first appeared in *Genii*, December 2000. *What's the Big Idea* first appeared in *At Guelph*, October 2003. *In the Moment* was first presented at the University of Guelph, 2003. *Beautiful Things* first appeared in *ChildView*, 2010. *Face, Forgiveness and the Other* was first presented at the University of Oxford, 2010. *Networking 101* first appeared in *Lifetimes*, vol. 2, 2011. *The Unqualified Poor* was first published in *Monthly Developments Magazine*, 2012.

Cover: PAGECREATIVE.CA
Text design and typesetting: PAGECREATIVE.CA
Ink drawings by Gretchen Sankey

in·cre·ment. noun 1. something added or gained; addition; increase. 2. profit; gain. 3. the act or process of increasing; growth. 4. an amount by which something increases or grows. 5. one of a series of regular additions.

"The most political decision you make is where you direct people's eyes. In other words, what you show people, day in and day out, is political.... And the most politically indoctrinating thing you can do to a human being is to show him, every day, that there can be no change." —Wim Wenders, *The Act of Seeing*

CONTENTS

THE WONDER OF CONFUSING KNOTS AND SKIRTING CHAOS

While growing up I had the opportunity to live in various parts of the Near East due to my father's work. The Iran of the day was not treated like a pariah state and used to showcase its art and handicrafts as evidence of the richness of its centuries-old culture and history. Iran's handmade carpets are among the most exquisite in the world, not only because of their intricate designs and subtle colors but also because of the range and quality of the material that is used – all the way from wool to silk. Yet the most intriguing way to enjoy the beauty and quality of a carpet is to see it being made. The weavers sit in front of the loom with the carpet stretched on it as they weave the threads, tie the knots and then cut the yarn before repeating the process all over again. Experienced weavers have the image of the design imprinted in their minds and know how each knot in a seemingly messy jumble of thousands of individual knots is part of the design, which then becomes a thing of beauty.

The essays in this book by David Peck are like the knots of a handmade carpet; they seem to deal with disparate parts of life, yet when taken together somehow make sense and bring wonder and mystery into a world that at times seems confusing. David draws from his rich experience of being a father and husband, philosopher, electrician and magician. Somehow these have all contributed to the critical skills he needed to be a development professional. More importantly, David addresses the issue of change and wonders about the kind of world we dream about. He asks the most existential of questions about what in life really matters.

In my years of teaching students of international development who dreamed of changing the world, I often struggled with their expectation that I would provide them with formulas and templates that would identify what was wrong and then lead them to the solutions. How could I tell them that change is not a straight line between how things are and how they should be, with packaged solutions providing the means? The only approximation that comes somewhat close to how social change actually takes place comes from the complexity sciences in which the dynamics of turbulent systems resemble the messiness of human relationships, the struggles for power and limited resources and the constant search for security, all interwoven with dreams of a better life. Turbulent systems are not random but reveal complexity even as each element is subjected to violent forces that simultaneously push the system in different directions. In what seems like chaos, there are fundamental laws that regulate the system and cause it to move in specific directions. If these laws are understood, the power of turbulent systems can be harnessed to bring about significant change. As much as this model explains much of social reality, social systems are not always subject to the same exacting certainty of physical laws but are influenced by the complexity and frailty of human nature.

However, life is not random. One of the basic premises of Chaos Theory is that there are hidden patterns in what seem to be random behaviours and events. Fractals in geometry reveal intricate patterns in what may have seemed as unstructured as a jagged shoreline or random shapes in nature. Perceiving and understanding these patterns is fundamental to being a change maker. The dynamics of how these patterns come into existence reveal how even small changes can have significant impacts.

Herein lies mystery: that in the midst of seeming chaos is incredible beauty; that at a time when the complexity and bleakness of a situations belie any hope for change, we can see that small changes do make a significant difference.

While David is a philosopher and moves in the world of ideas and logic with ease, it is his sense of wonder in the real world that peels away the layers of mystery. The fourth-century thinker and theologian Gregory of Nyssa, living at a time when conflicting ideas trying to define and articulate the Mysterious often resulted in rigid dogma and the branding of heretics, wrote, "Concepts create idols; only wonder grasps anything." As you read this collection of essays, may David's sense of wonder be contagious and challenge you to see and experience life differently.

Rupen Das
Beirut, Lebanon

THANKS

"Don't walk behind me; I may not lead. Don't walk in front of me; I may not follow. Just walk beside me and be my friend."
—Albert Camus

There are a lot of individuals to thank for this little book project of mine. It wouldn't have been possible without so many significant people. And as it may be my first and only "real" book, I need to cover quite a few relational bases. My influences have been formative, engaging and mostly friendly. I have been mentored by many and am the sum of various relational parts.

James, thanks for pushing me to take the next step and for transforming the manuscript into a book. I do appreciate your friendship and generosity.

To Eden and Bruce, thanks for the sushi, the conversation, our shared love for film and the incomprehensible dialogue around financial markets. Still doesn't make much sense to me.

Jim, your invite to Eldoret, Kenya, in the late eighties has made all the difference. Truly a sign that the little things do indeed matter in ways we rarely imagine. The trip changed my life; thanks for convincing me to go.

Michael, what can I say but a heartfelt thanks for the listening ear over the past few years. It's so good, right, true and affirming to be able to share the ups and downs with someone who understands.

To my brother Stephen, thank you for your editorial eye and precise blue pencil. As a principal you are a manager of big ideas in small packages. Thank you for all that you do. I believe teachers are underpaid and that schools should be palaces. Keep planting seeds in the next generation of change makers.

My first introduction to Michael Polanyi came through Lance Muir, whose thoughtful and steady encouragement and consistent and helpful critique have been a welcome part of my education and writing. Thanks, Lance. You are a good friend.

Victor Shepherd's careful commentary along the way has proved stimulating and an important part of my philosophical development. Your friendship has been rewarding. Your openness, generosity and gracious approach will continue to influence my thinking and writing.

My undergraduate professors at York University, including Claudio Duran, Arnold Itwaru, Jean Saindon, Sam Mallin, Stuart Shanker and David Jopling, all played a significant role in my academic growth. These people are scholars of the most serious kind. A special thank you to Jean and Claudio for your close friendship and for introducing me to the discipline. You taught me how important a well-placed question really is.

Rupen Das deserves my hearty thanks and appreciation for writing the foreword to this book, and for taking the time to invest in others. I would not be where I am today without his invite to Humber College for a coffee the day he introduced me to my post-graduate work in international development. He is a gracious friend who is kind and always supportive.

And to Baxter Kruger, thank you for each and every large time we have shared together. You've changed the way I see the world. My gratitude runs wide and deep. I love you, brother, even if you are a "Confederate." You have taught me that there is no such thing as a mere mortal. Priceless.

Thank you to my dear friend Jay Sankey for companionship, consistent affirmation and always-welcome conversation. It is largely because of you that I find myself philosophizing about this and that. Iron sharpens iron to be sure. Aristotle was right. Friendship is without a doubt one of the best virtues anyone can possess.

Matt, we've shared some crazy, wonderful and ridiculous moments together. We have laughed louder and longer than most. Thanks for everything. You've been a loyal and marvellous friend. You've gone the extra mile for me many times and it has always been noticed and deeply appreciated.

My parents encouraged my passion for the spoken and written word. They taught me to love reading, for which I am very grateful. They were without a doubt two of the most hospitable people I have ever known. They instilled in me an appreciation for other people, places and things and for that I give thanks.

And to my children Spencer and Victoria, you challenge me and give me so many new experiences and opportunities each and every day. Thank you for your laughter, your ability and willingness to reflect and your questions. You do indeed know more than you can tell and you do understand.

Finally, I would like to thank Elizabeth. You continue to encourage me in all things and have selflessly taken the time to read much of what I write. You smile at my idiosyncratic behaviour, my sometimes-neurotic outlook and are often willing to entertain the philosophical tangents I find interesting. Without your love and care I would be less of a writer and a different person.

TO START

"A book must be an axe to the frozen sea that is within us." —Kafka

This is a book about change and ideas. It's about reaching out beyond our grasp. It's a reflection on knowledge, experience and how we see the world. I hope it will encourage those who read it to ask better questions and indeed to meaningfully consider what's next. The future, the "not yet," awaits.

I've enjoyed an eclectic past, and so I have written about what I've learned as a magician, philosopher, father, teacher, electrician and international development specialist. I have dabbled in just about everything. I have failed miserably in some respects and taken risks that I am for the most part pleased about. I am still learning how to make sense of my average, everyday experience.

I believe in freedom, choice and responsibility. I believe we should be digging deeper and we must go beyond scratching the surface in all that we do – love, politics, religion, play, sex, science and thought. The list is joyfully endless.

Life matters. People matter. Ideas are essential. Examined ideas even better.

Levinas said, "We are all responsible and I more than the rest." So I challenge you as you read on to consider what's next, what you will leave behind and who is around the corner, where you are going and who you will connect with in the near future. Splash here and there and watch the ripples multiply out beyond your own backyard. We are without a doubt defined by others around us.

Thankfully, life is about baby steps, incremental change and a love that can and does endure. Peace.

ONE

WHAT'S THE BIG IDEA

"Under capitalism people devour people. Under communism it's the other way around." —Emil Fackenheim

W hy did I choose to study philosophy? Why, after eighteen years of working in the "real" world, would I choose to leave the comfort of my complacent and often predictable lifestyle? A way of life that consisted of an hour and a half to two hours a day caught in traffic, forty-five to seventy-five phone calls a day, rushed, Rolaids-inducing business lunches, an overflowing inbox of poorly written e-mails, imaginary corporate fires and enough inane and idle chitchat to make living on the ninth level of Dante's Hell feel merely like enduring a bad comedian on amateur night at a local comedy club. And oh, yes, at least ten parking tickets a year. I left all this and a steady paycheque to pursue a professional career in the academic world. Some called it foolhardy. I called it liberation.

Voltaire said, "We use ideas merely to justify our evil and speech merely to conceal our ideas." It seems like a good thing to say. Techniques of persuasion, rhetoric and beautiful metaphors become the tools of modern-day sophists attempting to tweak and twist hearts, minds and imaginations. Political figures, writers, entertainers, ministers, artists and the media offer up ideas about life and how to see the world as if we were all eating at some kind of all-you-can-eat philosophical buffet of detached thoughts and ideas. Today's main course is rhetoric. In the same way, lifestyle advertising spouts its own mediated messages that should, at best, be seen as a muddy mixture of conflicting ideas, assumed premises and shoddy conclusions. Global village? Indeed.

The other day, I found out the hard way what Sartre meant when he said, "Hell is other people." Someone said to me, in a rather cold and condescending tone, after hearing I was pursuing a post-graduate degree in philosophy: "That and a quarter will get you a phone call." I left the room with the conversation ringing in my ears and wondered what that phone call might actually be like. What if I could make one all-important phone call? Who would it be? Christ, Plato, Descartes, Pascal, Gandhi? Or maybe Elvis? He might have a lot to say. I hear he was kind of chatty.

I'm a philosopher and I am proud of it. I spend my time reading, thinking and considering ideas. I do my best to examine, think and reflect. I get wound up when things are said that indicate a lack of reflection or consideration for the Other. I believe that, like the worthless, unexamined life, the unexamined idea is not worth having.

We're all philosophers on some level. We all have ideas about religion and politics. We all have some version of the afterlife or perhaps no version at all. We all speak from a point of view, share a not-so-common perspective and will wax poetic on any number of issues if motivated by enough pain, passion, alcohol or anger.

Ideas are important. In some respects, they're a given. They are as accessible and plentiful as the grains of sand on the gritty seashore of the imagination. That may be true. It may be an experiential fact. Is it true, however, that popular ideas are rarely put under the critical and philosophical microscope? Are the ideas of others challenged, criticized and reflected on? Can we say that, as active participants in a democratic society, we are willing and freely able to examine the ideas of others?

Many years ago, I spent four weeks in Southeast Asia, primarily in Cambodia – a country that is beautiful, mysterious and tragic. Over the past ten years, I have spent much time reading and thinking about the history of Cambodia and the plight of its people. Often referred to as the "sideshow" of the Vietnam War, this is a country that has been largely forgotten by the international community. Thousands dead from mindless, detached, video-game-like bombing, seven to ten million land mines lying dormant like raw and lethal tumours. These pernicious little anti-personnel mines almost outnumber the current population of the country. Designed to maim and not kill, they have inflicted a horrific degree of physical and psychological pain on small rural communities throughout the country. Genocide. Thirty years of civil war. A war crimes trial still pending. One in three dead as a result of an idea. An idea about Marxism that went horribly wrong – a hyper-communistic, intellectual, academic idea. Some sideshow.

It is precisely for this reason that I chose to study philosophy. I wanted to be able to stand on the other side of an idea and say with a great deal of historical and philosophical confidence that the idea must be examined and that it may be wrong. I had a deep desire to sharpen my skills as a critical thinker. I was and am still in search of first things. I am honing a keen interest in knowing exactly why it was I thought this was this and that was that. Roland Joffé, director of *The Killing Fields*, has said about the human condition:

> We're a strange animal, so often destroying what we love for selfish ends and yet tantalized by the sense that there are other choices if only we had the strength to make them. In the politics of four hundred years ago, we find the same questions we battle with today.

I agree.

Fifty years ago, a man by the name of Saloth Sar and a small group of Cambodian academics, many of them former schoolteachers, went to France on scholarships to study. They found themselves drawn to a radical form of Communism and quickly joined arms in a metaphorical and nationalistic embrace. They were a small group of thinkers with extreme, desperate ideas about their country and the way things ought to be. They attended lectures, wrote papers and smoked French cigarettes. Twenty-five years after graduation, Pol Pot and the other members of this group were responsible for the deaths of millions of Cambodians. Appalling, severe and reprehensible. They saw it as their duty to punish, indoctrinate, detain and transform their friends and family. Obedience was demanded; questions were ignored and brushed carelessly aside. Hatred and fear were the weapons of this ideological regime. Death and destruction were the results. Thirty-three percent of the population was wiped out. Disturbing numbers and frightening statistics merely approximate the violence and pain these sovereign tyrants rained down on their country. As detailed in Joseph Conrad's *Heart of Darkness*, we can cry with those who survived and with the spirits of those who died: "The horror. The horror."

The Khmer Rouge were captured by an idea — a pernicious notion with brutal consequences. They were fascinated with power, infused with racism and bankrupt of any moral restraint. It has been noted that years before the regime was ruling Cambodia with lies, deception and the farmer's hoe, Pol Pot had spent much time secluded in the famed temples of Angkor Wat reading and studying *Mein Kampf*. Hitler's evil and inhumane doctrine influenced the lives of millions of others years later and a half a world away. One maniacal madman nurturing the other.

Ideas must be examined. They must be challenged and sometimes they must be subverted. I will continue to examine, think and reflect. I encourage everyone to do the same because I believe a degree in philosophy and a quarter will get you a whole lot more than a phone call. Thinking philosophically cultivates an inquisitive spirit. It encourages the formulation of relevant, important questions. It enables one to choose and to choose with informed conviction. And it fosters an analytical and pensive heart.

I am, however, open to the possibility that I may be wrong. If I am, perhaps you might find it useful to consider the existential implications the next time you drop a 25-cent coin into a pay phone and imagine this is it – your last conversation.

TWO

STUNG

"Globalization is a fact of life, but I believe we have underestimated its fragility." —Kofi Anan

To say the day was hot is an understatement. But the heat was a welcome reprieve from the searing stench of refuse. Sitting precariously on the back of a motorbike, in sandals and a helmet, neither of which fit me well, my tour guide and friend Romanea steered us to our final destination: Stung Meanchey.

Beyond the Royal Palace, the Silver Pagoda and its Emerald Buddha (dating from the seventeenth century), the National Museum and Wat Phnom, lies one of Phnom Penh's lesser-known landmarks: the garbage dump. Cambodia, like many countries in the global south, has neighbourhoods of slums sitting adjacent to industrial, medical and personal refuse. Stung Meanchey is one such place.

Covering a hundred acres of Phnom Penh's soil, it is a literal sea of garbage. Approaching the dump, I felt like a bizarre tourist, an out-of-place intruder. This wasn't a zoo or a freak show, after all, but real life. The homes, many of which would hardly pass for shacks, were built on stilts within and surrounding the dump proper. Driving deeper into the "town" and gaining a closer vantage point, I realized the houses were made with reclaimed materials found in the piles that formed Stung Meanchey, a place nearly ten thousand people call home.

In the distance I could see the inhabitants rummaging through piles of waste searching for recyclables and treasures to exchange for cash. With so many people constantly moving and working through the mountains of trash, the landscape looked as though it were a living, breathing thing. I learned that a successful day's work here (often more than twelve hours of hard labour) – where one met with rusting metal, broken glass, garbage and even hazardous medical waste – could yield about two thousand Cambodian riel, the equivalent of about $.50 American. I could hardly take it all in: the sights, sounds and smells of life in the dump.

It wasn't until we had dislodged our bike from the muddy refuse in front of a large truck being driven by an irate worker and continued our journey deep into the field of waste that I realized many of the workers, mostly women and children, were running around barefoot. Young children rushed to swarm onto the backs of trucks as they entered the dump, eager to claim the new load of garbage as their own. Clearly a premium was placed on fresh arrivals.

Walking deeper into Stung Meanchey, our feet covered in a sticky tar-black substance, and sinking into garbage nearly to our ankles, we met three women heading out to work in the dump. Despite their exhaustion – it was obvious they had already spent most of the day scavenging – they smiled at us through their *kramas* (scarves). Barefoot and bags in hand, the women each held a small metal hook, a handmade tool to help them sift through the garbage. I wanted to take their picture, to capture their truth, but I didn't have the courage to ask, though I'm sure from their kind and gentle demeanour that they would have allowed it.

Leaving the smoke and burning garbage behind, Romanea and I found a path that slowly led us out of the dump. There we met with a new truth: wealth, luxury and excess. The opulence of the Buddhist temples we were approaching was evident in both their grandeur and design. So much money spent on these places of worship, and yet so little for the people living in their shadows. It was only once the dump was behind us that Romanea confided he had worried for our safety. I couldn't help but wonder about the safety of those living in the dump.

What does their future look like? Who is taking care of them? Does the injustice of inequality – of opulence juxtaposed against extreme poverty – not make people stand up and demand action? But because Cambodia is just another struggling country, and Stung Meanchey just another dump, I assumed that no one else was angered by the injustice. While I was leaving the dump, a sign for the People Improvement Organization (PIO) outside a school caught my attention. I took note and decided to contact them when I returned home.

Phymean was born in Kampong Cham province. She has worked with many different international development groups, including the United Nations, but is now living out her dream of helping women and children at risk in the heart of Cambodia.

One afternoon while eating her lunch by the side of the Mekong River, Phymean was approached by a group of eager children who asked her for some money. They were hungry. When she had finished her meal, Phymean tossed the chicken bones aside and watched in horror as the boys and girls scrambled for the leftovers. She was astounded as the children sucked what little meat was left off of the bones. She quickly called them over. They sat down and formed a circle on the grass. She bought them a full chicken to share together and it was there, by the Mekong that a conversation began that changed her life. Clearly relationships make all the difference in the world. Food wasn't the only thing these kids couldn't afford. Subsistence living doesn't allow for luxuries like basic primary education – the second of eight UN development goals.

In 2002, she resigned from her full time job and started the People Improvement Organization (PIO) with aspirations of opening support offices in Canada, Australia, Europe and the USA. PIO's focus is to provide non-formal education and livelihood training to marginalized groups and to build the capacity of indigenous staff in order to nurture and develop future leaders within Cambodia. Phymean will tell you that "in Cambodia school is not free; the students must pay the teachers a *study fee.*" This is precisely why so many boys and especially girls will not be able to finish a basic primary education. Why they can't escape their realities in the dump.

Phymean and the PIO are indeed right in the middle of it all. Phymean will also tell you that one of the most important lessons she ever learned from her mother was how essential an education actually is. And she wants people from all over the world to stand beside the Cambodians in the dump. While they are not advertised on their website, the PIO does have volunteer opportunities for those who want to help make a difference. Offering three- to six-month internships in Stung Meanchey as well as shorter trips, Phymean is passionate and committed to equipping others to help change the realities of life in the dump. Phymean is fighting and advocating for sustainable change of all kinds. She is involved and she is making a difference.

Visiting Stung Meanchey, meeting people who live there and encountering those, like Phymean, who are trying to make a change, are priceless experiences. They are stark reminders of everything that is wrong with the world and the opportunities for each of us to create a positive change. How can we let this go on? How can the world turn a blind eye to thousands of individuals living in a garbage dump? How can this be acceptable?

The reality of Stung Meanchey causes me to reflect on the need for a better and more comprehensive vision of globalization. Surely it is evidence that the current approach is fundamentally flawed. It is places like Stung Meanchey that should compel us to explore innovative ways to create local and global change.

Together we can envision and develop a more equitable approach to how we view and treat others. Together we have the power to make a positive change – if we want to.

THREE

THE UNKNOWN REBEL

"We have sealed ourselves away behind our money, growing inward, generating a seamless universe of self." —William Gibson

There's nothing like a good cliché. Sure, we try to avoid them like the plague, but still they seem to creep up on us each and every day. *Things will never change. You can't teach an old dog new tricks. If it ain't broke, don't fix it. It's my way or the highway. It's too little, too late. We missed the window of opportunity. There are two sides to every story.* And my personal favourite, *It is what it is.* What exactly does that last one mean anyway? I can't think of a better way to say nothing. It is a verbal shrug that says you'll simply accept that things won't ever change because you're just too bone lazy to do anything about it.

Each of these clichés has a pejorative tone. They speak of defeat, fear and a complacent willingness to accept things the way they are. But it doesn't have to stay this way. We do have examples of those who made significant change. Like Rosa Parks, Martin Luther King or the the Unknown Rebel. Ordinary people who decided to stop doing nothing and embraced active change.

The Unknown Rebel is a nineteen-year-old man who went to the market and changed history. Many believe his name was Wang Welien. We don't know much about him – if he was socially awkward or if he would have sat in the back row of a church service or if he rarely put his hand up in class. What we do know is that in his ordinariness, in his shopping, he made an extraordinary contribution.

You see, Wang wasn't just some guy walking home from any market – he was in Tiananmen Square when the Chinese military invaded a non-violent student uprising in June of 1989. The tanks, in a violent response, rolled in to squash the students. Wang walked, clutching his white bag, in front of the line of Communist tanks. They moved left. He walked to their left. They swung to the right and Wang skipped to their right. Wang wouldn't let the tanks pass. A lone shopper on his way home from the market. He made his point. And he embraced active change to show this.

Wang, the Unknown Rebel, confronted the tanks where Mao had proclaimed a People's Republic in 1949. He walked on the Avenue of Eternal Peace, right next to the Forbidden City and the Gate of Heavenly Peace. The Great Hall of the People, the Museum of the Chinese Revolution and the Mao Tsetung Mausoleum consume most of Tiananmen's southern edge. I've walked the square. It's breathtaking. I almost tripped over the irony.

The philosopher Heraclitus said, "You can't step in the same river twice." The river will change, regardless of what we want. He saw change as constancy. Not so for Wang, whose actions were not passive – not constant – but rather the result of a conscious decision to make a passionate, committed difference. Did Wang realize the power of his actions? The power of the image of his walk home from the market? We may never know, but we can stand to learn from him. We can decide to stop doing nothing.

Rosa Parks, Martin Luther King Jr., Wang Welien. These are people who appreciated that little things can make a big difference. They realized that details matter, and that everything is connected. Like children, these individuals personify growth and change. But we, who accept things as they are, have lost this childlike spirit of hope and wonder.

As perpetual seekers, children are interested in everything and deterred by very little. My son Spencer, on seeing water swirl down the drain, asks, "Do we get that water back?" A passionate spirit engaged by wonder, Spencer lacks guile and a cynical edge. Instead, he finds delight in the everyday. He sees change as possible. He creates change. This is the committed and focused response to everyday ordinariness that makes it all extraordinary. This is the essential edge necessary for a change of heart, soul and mind.

Change is inevitable. But why stay static as it happens around you? Instead, why not create it? Grab it. Shape it. Mould it into something positive that only you can sculpt. Rosa Parks sat at the front of the bus. Martin Luther King Jr. shared his dream. Wang was out shopping. Remember, it is what you make it.

FOUR

STANDING ON THE EDGE

"The talk was still going on when, quite suddenly, a young violinist appeared on a balcony above the courtyard. There was a hush as, high above us, he struck up the first great D minor chords of Bach's Chaconne. All at once, and with utter certainty, I had found my link with the center." —Werner Heisenberg

I wrote this essay because I believe in wonder and because I love watching and performing a beautiful piece of sleight-of-hand magic. I have spent about thirty-two years in the business but often have been dissatisfied with the long-term lack of artistic edge in the craft. My frustration drove me to reflect on whether or not magic is an art form, why wonder comes and goes and how I might be able to reconcile the gap between what it is and what I hoped it might be.

I had grown up believing that it was indeed an art form of the most serious kind. Many magicians often referred to playing cards as if they were keys on a piano. Didn't take long before I began to question the analogy and felt somewhat betrayed. I'm still living in a hopeful place between art and craft. I trust you will find a conversation here that is applicable to other areas and ways of life.

So you think that's art. Art is subjective, you say. What individuals deem art is specific. Specific to cultural, societal and personal norms. Relativism rules in the world of art. What I like, you may not like and vice versa. I might walk out of a film; you, however, might recommend it to all your family and friends.

It seems to me that these truisms with respect to the art world are accepted by many on most levels of society. Each one of us views a piece through our own world and our own eyes. We wear individual, cultural, emotional and relational sunglasses. These tinted eyepieces affect the way we see, and yet we often do not see exactly how they affect what we see – a tacit filter that influences each work of art and its interpretation and yet transcends our explicit awareness.

The way we see the world around us clearly affects how we interpret a work of art. Individual experience will either add to or detract from any implicit interpretation. If the perception of art is in fact a truly relative experience and subject to one's interpretation (as so many preach and live), then how does one ever condescend to call a piece either good or bad? By what criteria does one approach a work in question and critically proceed? Implicit within the subjective stance resides the notion that art cannot be defined. It suggests that art is simply open to interpretation. Art, it would seem, can never be judged. Perhaps a simple like or dislike towards a piece would be sufficient within this supposedly subjective and interpretative milieu. To suggest that one work of art is better than another is just plain foolish. Merely claiming that one piece has inherent qualities about it that are more endearing, more challenging to the eye or more stimulating to the soul is to suggest that art is anything but a subjective experience. The implication is that, perhaps, an overarching sense of what art is exists somewhere. Individually or collectively, on some intellectual, emotional or maybe even spiritual level, a paradigm is assumed. These axiomatic assumptions about art question and ultimately negate the subjective approach. To deny this is to be relegated to a simple "Yes, I like it" or "No, I don't." In my world, a specific piece may be seen as brilliant, or even a work of genius, but to you it may be nothing more than a piece of self-indulgent trash.

We seem to speak from a subjective framework and yet paradoxically we judge a work from some sort of objective reference point. Relatively speaking we objectively denounce or praise. And so we all continue to expound about art as subjective experience all the while claiming qualitative rights about this piece or that. This is, to be sure, ironic - an artful contradiction.

Definition must then precede. Perhaps the question is not what is the right definition, but what is the best definition? William Faulkner speaks with concision. He implies that a work of art will have a life of its own. He speaks of intention. He reminds us of the potential gift of an artist's work. He wishes for longevity, stimulation and soul.

> The aim of every artist is to arrest motion, which is life, by artificial means and hold it fixed so that a hundred years later, when a stranger looks at it, it moves again since it is life. Since man is mortal, the only immortality possible for him is to leave something behind him that is immortal since it will always move. This is the artist's way of scribbling Kilroy was here on the final and irrevocable oblivion through which he must someday pass.

Before proceeding I wish to make the reader explicitly aware of my position. This is an essay on magic, magic as art. Is it or is it not an art form? The question of whether or not magic falls into the category of a performance art is a question, that for the time being, I will leave for others.

My intention is to ask questions and to begin a serious dialogue about a craft that I love. Perhaps "love" is too strong. I have a strong passion for magic. Sleight of hand makes me smile. The work behind an effect is often my driving force, and I believe it is precisely this for which I have such profound affection. I enjoy performing, watching and talking about magic. Some of my closest friends are magicians. There is nothing quite like the feeling of walking off a stage to serious, affirming and engaging applause. For me, the adrenaline rushes through my body and for a brief moment I am transported elsewhere. So you see, plain and simple, I am very fond of magic. And if at any time this paper seems judgmental or academically harsh in any way, please remember my affection. I have taken off my sunglasses (seemingly) and am making an attempt at serious interaction with the notion of magic as art. I hope to promote a discussion and to involve others in an ongoing debate. I wish to raise some questions, start a dialogue and consider the implications.

Magic, it seems to me, wants to be art; it desperately wants to be art. Ask a magician and she will call herself an artist. Ask me and I am not so sure. Art should engage, it should question, it should remind, it should seek and it should "arrest motion." As a magician, all too often I am reminded of the mortal effect of the effect. The wonder is entertained for a brief moment and is quickly forced outside of the soul in favour of the methodology. "Wow! How did you do that? That's amazing! Can I see those cards? The hand really is quicker than the eye." Innocently enough the spectator moves to the question of how and not why. Within seconds the audience focuses on the technique. Pushed from wonder to wondering.

Bombarded with answers in a culture that is primarily interested in solutions, the wonder of a simple coin vanish is trampled beneath our empirical sensibilities. What might be a moment of focus on art is often reduced to nothing more than an intriguing puzzle. The puzzle might look difficult the first time around, but at the end of the day, a solution is not only impending but we have been taught to believe that it is inevitable. And so the wonder is drowned in the solution, literally and metaphorically. Wonder is the goal and yet the solution seems to prevail.

Jeff McBride in a February 1998 interview in *Magic* said, "You can look at a painting and you don't have to know what pigments and brush strokes went into it to be able to appreciate and enjoy it." I agree and will take this a step further. I am suggesting that if and when the pigment or the strokes become the focus then the piece has shifted in its function. The technique of an artist can be appreciated and admired on some level and at some point must be appreciated in this way, but clearly technical fascination only requires the participant's cursory attention. To reduce art to its functionality is to cloud and redirect the poetic intentionality.

Magic, in order to be art, has to be about so much more than technique, skill and dexterity. Good art does not pull us towards the technique but towards the experience. Magic and its wonder, however, are often quickly vilified in favour of the inherent technique. With this impression of technique and skill left with the viewer, a magician's abilities or a magician's art is judged on her skill, not necessarily on her ability to engage or to promote wonder. Motion may be arrested for a moment, but is quickly lost within the method. For this reason I believe magic is more like an imprint than a voice. It seems to lack a certain staying power – *Rambo* vs. *Raging Bull*. It has a beauty to it but nevertheless it doesn't seem to have the ability to stay with you for a very long time. It lacks any serious skill with respect to resonation. It may impress and may even arouse, but does it ferment?

Without question there is a relationship between art and craft. The technique is the medium. Clearly, then, the piece and thereby its message is communicated through and is directly linked to the technique of the artist. But in order for the work to be effective, this can only be purely incidental. Alexander Solzhenitsyn said that "the task of the artist is to sense more keenly than others the harmony of the world, the beauty and the outrage of what man has done to it, and poignantly to let people know." If this is the case, then surely the technique can only be the messenger. It is obliged to remain hidden. It must situate itself in the background as the artist speaks to each and every person who partakes. The language of a great artist is not spoken through her tenacious and passionate technical abilities, but through her heart, her intention and her soul.

Perhaps this has something to do with the immediacy of the image: the visual. The image has a power and a beauty to it that requires focus. It often engages and interacts and yet it is usually forgotten by the fresh and ever more engaging Polaroid our eyes turn to next, a PowerPoint presentation of ideas that is all about the moment and rarely about reflection. Enticing, but immediately replaced by this image or that. It is like an odour that invades a room. It overwhelms your senses but then is quickly and effectively ushered out by a fresh, new and ever more pervasive, pleasant breeze. The wonder of the effect or the efficacy of the image is trampled beneath a methodological focus as the spectator cries, "Show me that again!" unconsciously saying to herself, "Maybe this time I will see how it's done."

I have often wondered if Doug Henning has had an impact on the public's understanding of how magic is perceived. For all the good and positive movements he made and for all he contributed to the craft, to what degree did he further a methodological focus by constantly referring to magic as an "illusion"? By constantly reminding his television and live audiences that it was just an "illusion," he implied that the magic had nothing to do with what was happening right before their "very eyes." An illusion has a viable explanation whereas magic does not. A magician wishes to hear people say, "I don't believe it." However, when the perception has shifted and the notion of an "illusion" has been reinforced, they may say, "I don't believe it, but it's merely an illusion." The implication is that there must be an explanation. Wouldn't it be ironic for all of Henning's focus on "wonder," if he furthered on some subconscious level the mechanics of the illusion? Implicitly the audience has been drawn away from the wonder in an attempt to solve the illusion or visual puzzle.

Magic leads to disbelief and disbelief to wonder. "Illusions," however, lead to questions, and questions often lead to a desire for answers and solutions – not more questions. We live in an age that loves solutions. We need to know. And once we know, we no longer question. Is not the wonder found in the question? We wonder when we ask. "It's the question that drives us, Neo," said Trinity in the one of 1999's most insightful films, *The Matrix*. By asking more questions and by asking them often we will find ourselves in a perpetual state of wonder. Questions lead to growth and insight. Answers, it seems to me, often breed complacency and mediocrity. When we know, we feel as if we have arrived. We roll over on our pillow, change the channel and go back to sleep. There is no longer any need for fascination with the question. Talk to children. "Why is the sky blue?" they will ask. "Why do candles burn?" "How come our God is the true God?" "Why do we cry?" And so on.

I am reminded of a truly wonderful experience a few years ago after coming off stage and greeting a friend after a show. She had brought a young boy along with her to the afternoon performance and he had to meet the magician. After having our picture taken together, I chatted to him for a few minutes and I gave him one of the coins I had produced during my version of the Miser's Dream. He was visibly thrilled. I left that day feeling pleased and never gave it much more thought. Weeks later I found out that this young man had taken the "magic" coin I had given him, had it encased in plastic and slept with it under his pillow. Was he concerned about the method? Did he find the technique fascinating in any way? All that mattered to him was that he had in his possession some sort of magical instrument. Sure, he may have asked "How?" but he made room for the magic and the wonder grew.

Answers may be necessary, but are they not a strong impediment to wonder? The recent fascination with unraveling the puzzle of Erdnase seems to support this. I understand why historians and scholars are working through this question, but what are the implications? The legend of Erdnase is far more wonderful and magical than the potential outcome of this academic exercise. The mystery is the legend. The wonder is found within the notion of not really knowing for sure. It's wonderful precisely because we do not know. We need to have a clear understanding of history, but what will be the cost to our ability to wonder?

T. Nelson Downs in *The Art of Magic* spoke prophetically about the loss of wonder in a scientific age. In 1980 the "King of Koins" had concerns about where we were headed with respect to magic and its common perception. He felt that technology and its effects would seriously undermine the ability of magic to promote wonder within the spectator:

>...when the positive and negative poles of an electro-magnet hold the human body in space some genius will have invented a machine capable of perpetual motion and some alchemist will have discovered the secret of transmitting the baser metals into gold. In such an age of real wonders mere magic will not be tolerated.

Written three years after Einstein first published his early work on the Theory of Relativity, it isn't surprising that Downs wondered about the future of "mere magic." Arthur C. Clarke echoes this sentiment when he claims that "smoothly functioning technology gives the appearance of real magic." The question that is raised as a result of these statements is simply this: As we make such fantastic technological leaps, can an individual experience of wonder survive? Science and the progress it has enjoyed has taught us to love and to believe in the answer. Everything has a solution. Our love for the narrative structure of story and of life only seems to support this claim. The scientific tradition assumes that one day we will have it all figured out. The wonder of life and of magic is buried somewhere beneath this pervasive pursuit of empirical knowledge. The all-important end vilifies the means. Whatever happened to the wonder filled journey?

One of the reasons I believe that magicians do not question their craft is because they have already decided that magic is art. Their conclusion has been drawn; their answer is clear. The analogy of the symphony or of the classical musician is often used in an attempt to argue that magic is in fact an art form. Please remember I believe that it may be, but this analogy is misleading at best.

Roger Klause's wonderful book is titled *In Concert*. The symphonic analogy is used throughout. Similarly, Gary Kurtz suggests that the moves in magic are like the notes in music. This musical analogy is effective precisely because it appeals to magicians on an emotional level. We all want to think of ourselves as great composers. We all hope to be seen as great artists. However, to suggest that the same amount of work, sweat and soul went into the Misers Dream as into Debussy's "Reverie" seems misguided and artistically unfair. Classical music and its composition is not analogous to magic and the sleight of hand that is behind it. For this to be the case, the two comparisons would need more experiential congruency. This they do not have. They both require practice, discipline and an adherence to technique, but what about the outcome? Using and accepting this analogy presupposes that the two disciplines are synonymous in every way. It is a logical fallacy to equate the two. It sounds good in an argument and appeals to us on several levels, but it is misleading and encourages a complacent understanding of magic as art. Can the Chinese Linking Rings evoke the same reaction as one of Mozart's favourite pieces? Have you ever seen someone moved to tears after the most engaging of magic shows? Revisit these questions and perhaps you will see where the analogy breaks down.

Consider other art forms. Great literature of hundreds and even thousands of years ago still speaks to us today. The books may be old and worn, the poems may seem tired and cliché, and yet they resound within bedrooms, universities and the naked hearts of innocent lovers. Lost within the words, they gaze into each other's eyes and are profoundly touched by the artist. "Only the poets can really see the stars," said Emerson. Agree or disagree? Painters, poets, writers, filmmakers, sculptors and composers may have a key to the cosmos that others do not. I wonder what the stars look like immediately following or even years after the most beautiful rendition of a classic magical effect like Triumph, a Matrix coin assembly, the Gypsy Thread or maybe even moments after a Lear Jet vanishes right before your very eyes? Out of this world? I think not.[1]

My experience of what I would call great art is rarely reduced to technique. Consider the novel *Frankenstein*, a touching reminder of humanity facing the demon of technology. Shelley speaks to the human condition and leaves us with a compelling story, but also implores us to beware. Scorcese's *Raging Bull* consciously studies the dark corners of the human soul. Issues of love, hate, ego and self-control are consistently and vividly portrayed throughout the film. Questions are raised that affect each and every one of us, questions that may not be easily answered, questions that require serious reflection. The filmmaker responsibly encourages us to ponder, monitor and perhaps even alter our relationships to the world and to those around us. Plato's *Republic*, Beethoven's "Moonlight Sonata," Yeats's "The Second Coming" and van Gogh's "Starry Night" are all examples and reminders of "arrested motion." Do we find ourselves asking the same questions of Monet's brush or of Shakespeare's pen as we do of the magician's hands? Clearly, they too are masters of a sleight of hand of sorts, but their methods do not seem to overwhelm the outcome or the individual intention of a piece.

Speaking to us years later, their power resides in their voice. Imprints they are not. Time, appreciation and their social and philosophical effect have confirmed this is the case.

There is no doubt that magic captures something. But once the initial gift has been unwrapped, does it keep on giving? It may even have a timeless quality that suggests it has a life of its own, but is it art? Walker Percy described the work of an artist to an interviewer in these words:

> My theory is that the purpose of art is to transmit universal truths of a sort, but of a particular sort, that in art, whether it's poetry, fiction or painting, you are telling the reader, or the listener, or the viewer something he already knows, but which he doesn't quite know that he knows. So that in the action of communication, he experiences a recognition, a feeling that he has been here before, a shock of recognition. And so what the artist does or tries to do is simply to validate the human experience and to tell people the deep human truths which they already unconsciously know.

To be sure, magic is a craft, perhaps more, but to assume it is an art form without questioning its conclusions is misguided and culturally naïve. Magic seems to be solely interested in gratification rather than edification. Its innate egocentricity may be its biggest downfall. Good art, it seems to me, must be so much more than just entertainment. It is a bridge to an artist's eyes and soul. It enables those who partake to actively participate in someone else's five senses. Good art is like a room full of doorways, each one potentially leading us to a world of emotions and knowledge and experience. Its function or utility is found in its ability to engage. Perhaps magic's greatest virtue is to promote wonder.

All art has a social responsibility, not only to the artist but also to those who receive it. It must be involved in a relationship that is alive. It must give and it must take. Maybe these questions must be asked of all art: How does this make me a better person? Will I love more? Will I hate less? Do I smile with every breath I take?

Diane Ackerman, in *A Natural History of the Senses*, writes, "it is the province of art to throw buckets of light into the shadows and make life new again." I believe that it is fundamentally important to ask this question of magic. And we should ask it often, the bucket gripped in one hand and the pack of cards held loosely in the other.

As we continue to make an attempt at scribbling "Kilroy was here," as we hope to "transmit universal truths of a sort," may I remind you that in many ways the deck has been stacked against us.

FIVE

ON THE HOOK AT BARK LAKE

"All that you can take with you is that which you have given away."
—Sign on George Bailey's bank wall in *It's a Wonderful Life*

Minding my business while taking care of business, Jack shouted, "Come on, David, we have to go." Jack's a venture capitalist. He's made lots of money taking risks on interesting people and ideas. His free market antennae clearly couldn't sense the urgency with which I was answering this important call of nature. Emptying my bladder next to the pine tree, I thought of a highschool teacher who told me to pee on my hands and feet to deal with calluses – sound advice for those with tough, unforgiving skin. "David, let's go," he shouted. I zipped up, spun around and moved towards the frantic voice by the edge of the lake. Jack and Duane were scrambling to get the boat into the water. I could hear shouting in the distance. We were in a big hurry. On the horizon it looked like someone was going under for the third or fourth time. His name was Omar. He was a nice guy about twenty-five years old. His buddy on a nearby shore started to swim towards his terrified, drowning friend. In an instant our trip took on new life and became an experience that none of us was prepared for, but in which we all knew exactly what to do. We didn't know who he was, where he was from or what he believed in. What mattered most was this man's life. The bass would have to wait.

Michael and Woody had left our expedition early. They were heading to the other side of the lake. Michael was schooled in business and trained as a pastor. We laugh often about how he should have spent more time in the arts and less time with religious folk and numbers. And how can you not like a guy named Woody? His body language spoke of sage advice and Socratic wisdom. It surrounded him like a warm winter coat. When we told Michael and Woody our story later, they were shocked. From their perspective it looked like we were merely hacking around. Indeed. They had no idea the imperative we were working under.

What an eclectic group of men. A gaggle of goons, we would be called in some circles – a chef, a pastor, a philosopher, a venture capitalist and Woody. Two odd couples plus one. Sounds like the makings of a Wes Anderson film. Saturday Night Live might be interested.

I jumped into the centre of the aluminum craft and assumed a position of power. I swear I heard someone shout, "Steady as she goes." Jack was navigating as I ploughed full steam ahead without looking behind me. The oars were splintery and short. They refused to stay in the brackets. The metal pins kept popping up and out. The centre was not holding. I thought about the painful, rubbery blisters that would appear on my hands the next day. The boat looked and felt like it had carried a dead body or two over the years. The holes, dents and freshly spun spider webs were evidence of the stories attached to our dubious craft. I thought of my father's favourite expression: "Worse things happen at sea." I noticed two holes in the bottom of the boat and for a moment I wondered about the direct shotgun blast fired off during a careless hunting party. The rescue craft used by many and cared for by few. The water was coming in at an uncomfortable pace. It was a concern for all of us who hadn't changed into appropriate footwear for a trip like this.

Duane, a master chef and kitchen utensil salesman, was bailing with a cracked cranberry juice container. He always had something funny to say. I don't remember anything rolling off his tongue this time. Right then he was making sure we stayed afloat. The chunks of Styrofoam and plastic bags just weren't doing the trick. The lake was seeping in.

Our destination was clear. A life depended on us.

Within minutes we had Omar hooked onto the back of the boat. He had just enough energy to hold on tight. His friend trailed behind, caught up and grabbed on as well. The back of the boat was sinking low. I could barely row.

We made it back to shore. The would-be swimmers were full of thanks and the boat of water. Omar stood with his hands on his knees, bent over, embarrassed and out of breath. He was spent. He smiled and thanked us profusely. Tom filled us in. It was a classic case of a distance looking shorter than it actually was. Omar went for broke and was overcome with unexpected exhaustion. The objective looked manageable, but he soon found out how a little foresight might have made all the difference. This was a deserted lake by all accounts and we were the only other visitors there all day. We arrived at the exact time we were needed. I never did ask Jack what the venture capitalist would say about odds like these. I'm not a gambler, but I do like metaphors. Life is full of them. In our case it was just beyond the shore – fishers of men, a boat full of holes, a drowning stranger, bailing water and swimming the distance. Did I mention we didn't bring along life jackets for this portion of our trip? Camus would be thrilled with the irony.

Later that night we talked about it under the stars over port and cigars. We may have saved Omar's life, but he did us a favour as well.

We exchanged hellos with the two of them from a distance. No formal greetings. No handshakes.

As we were talking among ourselves, Jack interrupted our post mortem and yelled out, "Hey, what's your name?" "Omar," he shouted back. "Nice to meet you," we all responded.

A grace full day on Bark Lake – one that Omar will be forever thankful for and one we will never forget.

SIX

TO SEE

"Ah, but a man's reach should exceed his grasp, or what's a heaven for?" —Robert Browning

Call it vision casting, blue-sky thinking, or maybe even innovation. Call it the ability to see or anticipate that which has not yet been realized. Regardless, what we're talking about is having the ability to harness the power of your thinking today in order to crystallize it into action for tomorrow.

Vision. What does the word conjure up for you? Notions of clarity, perhaps: a clean windshield on your newly washed car; enjoying a clear blue day from the sky bridge of the Petronas Towers in Kuala Lumpur; looking out at the horizon from Senggigi Beach on the shores of Lombok; standing on the edge of the Great Rift Valley; wandering the stone-chiselled halls of Angkor Wat; or skiing the snow-covered slopes of Whistler? In each of these scenarios, the world stretches out before you in a horizon that can never be met.

The word *vision* has been around for some time now. The *Oxford English Dictionary* tells us its origin was around the late thirteenth century from the Anglo-French word *visioun* or *visio*, translated as the "act of seeing" or plainly "to see." Perhaps you define vision as simply being able to see it all, a gift many of us take for granted. Looking out at our surroundings. Taking a hard look within ourselves. God is in the details, after all. To be simple and clear, sometimes vision is all about stopping dead in our tracks, bending down to smell the flowers and looking a little closer.

Recalling the work of Lao Tse, Julie Dupré once wrote, "The reality of a hollow object is in the void and not in the walls that define it." Lao was speaking, of course, of spiritual realities, as many architects might suggest. "These are the realities also of the Petronas Towers. The power of the void is increased and made more explicit by the pedestrian bridge that ... with its supporting structure creates a portal to the sky ... a door to the infinite."[1] A door to the infinite? Architecture that casts a vision. Inspiring and challenging words. No wonder vision statements have gained such tremendous weight in the business world. Designed to drive organizations, vision statements are meant to represent a set of shared dreams, goals and aspirations of founders, boards, employees and executives alike. But, if we are to look closer at what vision casting, thinking and statements are all about, we might find another story.

Recently I have been working with a company called Soul Systems,[2] a consulting firm that works with various types of leaders, helping them to frame the present and the future of their organizations. Soul Systems has a simple vision, and it's being fulfilled. Director Jonathan Wilson asks his clients very relevant questions, including: When you read your company's vision statement, does it have power over you? Does the vision it point to compel you and draw you back again and again to dream of new possibilities? Jonathan writes, "Vision statements in companies today are too often the result of dutiful exercise rather than the articulation of a genuine dream, held within the company, about what the future could look like. The statements that result from such exercises are often generic and dry; and rarely compelling." True vision, he reminds us, inspires, compels and sustains.[3]

Visionaries tend to be people who have idiosyncrasies and creative outlets that many of us can't even begin to understand. They are often people who are organized in their neurotic dis-organization. Some people even call them right brain thinkers. I, however, do not like this simple act of dividing one's natural faculties into left and right cerebral hemispheres. Taking the human brain and reducing it to compartments does not allow us to unpack the way we and others do what we do. It diminishes the impact of one's life and work into a simple question of anatomy. Furthermore, it immediately polarizes discussions into an "us" versus "them" mentality. It's divisive and exclusive kind of thinking like this that ultimately boxes us in. The rights and the lefts. In other words, some have it and some don't. I'm uncomfortable with this kind of deterministic approach to life's nuanced complexities. Exceeding our grasp is beyond the rights, lefts and undecideds. We are so often an intricate bundle of freedom, choice and responsibility. Throw a little paradox and contradiction into the mix as well. A composite of complexity.

In the book *The Little Prince,* Antoine de Saint-Exupéry shares a wonderful story about a six-year-old boy. In the opening of the book this young boy recounts an experience where he saw a "magnificent picture" in a jungle book called *True Stories.* In this storybook it was said that a boa constrictor can swallow their prey whole without even chewing. It's clear that this little boy is fasci-nated by the details. He is a wonder-filled child. Later in the story he tells us the snakes are not able to move after their large meals, and so they sleep during a six-month period of digestion. The little boy is so taken with this picture of the snake and its prey that he decides to draw what he "sees" – a snake digesting an elephant – clearly a fun and creative outlet for a young energetic and creative voice. In de Saint-Exupéry's classic we see the drawing. On the surface it does indeed look a little like a hat (see "drawing number one" below). This of course is all dependent on your perspective, as the boy finds out.

De Saint-Exupéry writes about how the young boy showed grown-ups around him the picture of his "masterpiece" and asks them if his drawings were scary. This is, after all, a six-year-old boy's image of a snake digesting an elephant. Proud of his work, he sees beyond the drawing and imagines great and wonderful things.

But the adults answered, "Why be scared of a hat?" Their comments perplex his young mind and he is astounded at their inability to "see" what he has seen, imagined and drawn. He quickly points out to them that his drawing is not a picture of a hat, but is a picture of the boa constrictor digesting an elephant. He's offended at their lack of vision and goes on to paint a picture for the reader of an adult world that has been poisoned by the cynicism of adulthood and the loss of wonder in the too often compartmental-ized "grown-up" mind. De Saint-Exupéry writes of the young boy: "The grown-ups advised me to put away my drawing of Boa con-strictors outside or inside and apply myself instead to geography, history, arithmetic and grammar. That is why I abandoned, at the age of six, a magnificent career as an artist."[4] The adults and their lack of vision shut this young boy down. He saw the world in a way that any visionary might and yet his desire for something other was stifled by structured and uninspired ideas.

Visionary thinking requires the ability to take risks. To situate ourselves in the here and now and yet be looking for what's next. Getting hypnotized by the task at hand will only get in the way of moving forward. And it's not movement for the sake of movement. Inanimate objects do that. Pool balls hitting other pool balls on a table create action. The questions are: What is the action being created? Is it impactful and does it have meaning? What I'm talking about here is movement forward, up and beyond. The next level is often beyond our grasp. Our awareness of its position is the first step towards getting there.

To cast a vision far, wide and deep, we are asked to take the necessary steps in order to make things happen. To dream one has to be asleep. True. However, in order to dream and act one must be awake, alive and ready. Those with vision do indeed dream, but visionary dreamers spend very little time sleeping, it seems to me. They do, act and make things happen. Part of visionary thinking, part of vision casting, requires us to be fully present and alert.

A lack of wonder and inability to see things in a clear, distinct and open structured manner led the adults in *The Little Prince* to foolishly suggest that the young boy put down his canvas and pick up his calculator. This uninspired thinking can only be seen as lost opportunity: What might have been in this boy's life if he had been allowed to pursue the life of an artist?

Inspire. Compel. Sustain.

And then share the picture of the future we seek to create as individuals and as communities.

Move out from the structure of the seemingly ordinary and everyday, and take the necessary risks to face your fears and truly inspire yourself to move beyond to what's next. The future is the not yet. Once you have taken the leap into this unknown, you will inspire others to do the same. Ask yourself questions often. And ask difficult ones even more often than that. What is it that is lying out beyond your grasp? I'm not talking about some kind of material or objectified idea of what success may or may not be. This isn't about mere success. Dollar figures and material value are not welcome here. They are the potential by-products of ideas, goals and outcomes that have been wrestled with and have been tried by the fire of experience. I'm talking about more than this simple attainment. This is, after all, about vision. Where can you take yourself, your family, your organization and your team?

To be a visionary requires a belief in change and a belief that change is possible. Yes, it may be incremental and it may come slowly. But taking a road less travelled means taking one's time and making the right choices along the way. Change is possible and it does indeed require a belief in ourselves and a need to not underestimate our abilities. Change is about hope and an expectation that tomorrow things will be different.

Luther Burbank, the famed botanist and horticulturist, was a visionary. A man who dreamed large and comprehensive dreams and yet was rooted enough to act and make things happen. He developed the freestone peach, the white blackberry and a spineless cactus. He created the Burbank potato in the late 1800s and later sold the rights for $150. The potato was more resistant to disease and was therefore exported to help Ireland recover from the Great Famine. The potatoes were dying. Something had to be done. Burbank had a vision to change potatoes for the better, and his end result has been a huge success. Today, Burbank's creation is the most widely cultivated potato in the US and McDonald's french fries are made exclusively from it.

Burbank was also very relational. He liked to hold parties and always asked his friends to sign his family guest book. Thomas Edison was visiting one evening and in the line next to his name, where the column read "personal interests," Edison wrote, "Everything." This is the passionate sprit we need to reawaken within ourselves if we are to become visionaries. Edison was a visionary precisely because he was present and in the moment.

He saw the value of, in short, everything. A wonderful anecdote to remind us all of our inability to see as a child might. The details for Edison mattered a great deal. He was a perpetual child at heart. Wonder was the driving force behind everything he did and yet it never got in the way of making important things happen.

This is the committed and focused attitude that is essential for a vision that looks forward, connects the dots while looking back and acts in the present with passion, vigour and conviction.

SEVEN

IN THE MOMENT

"The moment one gives close attention to anything, even a blade of grass, it becomes a mysterious, awesome, indescribably magnificent world in itself." —Henry Miller

I think, therefore I am. Descartes' celebrated philosophical statement. A profound proclamation that changed the way we see the world. By bringing reality into question he was able to doubt everything and assume the cogito. The cogito then became for Descartes the first thing – the place to start. He believed that he could erase all questionable knowledge and begin again. Existence was proven as a result of his ability to reason. Using this as the starting point, he could then rationally call everything into question and thereby acquire "true" knowledge.

I wonder, I think, therefore I am. What if Descartes had phrased and reflected upon his ontological notion in a different manner? What if his philosophy of mind and body had been informed by a holistic approach, on a level that included the body and its sense experience? His divisive approach leaves little room for an embodied response to the rich complexity of everyday experience. By omitting the body's experience of being in the world, he implicitly ignored an important and relevant aspect of the way we perceive the world.

Descartes' mechanistic interpretation and analysis of wonder does not allow for the nuances and subtleties of this, the most primitive passion.[1] How is it that the experience of wonder comes to an end? Can wonder linger and avoid an infiltration of reason? Does reason conflict with wonder? The experience of wonder must be viewed as an end in itself. To suggest that it is merely a means to a further and more practical end is to regulate and mediate the experience. If I am to dwell in wonder then I must do precisely that, dwell. To dwell is to be at home with an experience. Dwelling is "staying with" wonder. It is about pulling up a chair, finding a comfortable spot, residing and being.

Wonder for Descartes is the first of six passions. They are wonder, love, hatred, desire, joy and sadness. Wonder is an emotional response that is experienced as we are introduced to something new and unusual – something that we do not have an explanation for. Wonder is synonymous with surprise, or that which might be described as marvellous. It should be also noted that the passions of Descartes are said to be similar to our understanding of emotions today. It is interesting that he calls wonder the most "primitive" passion. This idea suggests that in Descartes' understanding, wonder is of secondary importance. The use of primitive here implies something that is underdeveloped or that lacks a clear and meaningful sophistication. Wonder assumes an inferior role. The question, however, is, an inferior role to what?

Wonder is a resonant, embodied and emotional response to that which is awe-inspiring, astounding or marvellous. This is my starting point. This is the first of many things. Via this working definition I am suggesting that my understanding of wonder is like a work in progress and it is under construction. Wonder is difficult to define, and to speak of it in any normative way suggests an over-simplification of what I believe is a rich and complex phenomenon.

To be sure, wonder is an emotional responsive arousal of a particular sort to something deeply surprising. Descartes writes that wonder is a "sudden surprise of the soul."[2] Consider its resonant presence in the descriptive statement "I gazed in wonder out and over the edge of the Great Rift Valley." The wonder of standing on the edge of something so unfamiliar, grand and overwhelming is to experience that which is wonderful. It inspires a sense of awe, and clearly one could speak of the soul being suddenly surprised by such a natural and yet seemingly unnatural phenomenon. Descartes and I agree on what wonder is. It is emotional and it does involve surprise. Where we differ, however, is with respect to the role of reason within all things wonderful. It seems to me that this emotional and sometimes momentary reaction or response is embodied and explicitly real. It is an expression of the relationship between a subject and an object. It can be an optional, inclusive and emotional response to one's everyday surroundings. When I wonder I am captured in a moment. In short, I am wonderstruck – emotionally arrested and enraptured in a moment and in the moment. However, when I reason, wonder is set aside. For Descartes, when wonder ceases knowledge begins.

Today the word *wonderful* has many uses and applications. It is used to describe experience, food and things that we consume. Vacations, films and conversations are often referred to as wonderful. To describe something in such an objective and what I will call meaningless way does not capture my intentions here. *Wonderful* is often used to merely mean "something or someone that is good or exciting or perhaps unique in some way." This trite use and expression of that which is wonderful lacks the kind of precision that I am looking for. When I refer to an experience as being wonderful, it is to say that my experience was full of wonder. Indeed it is to refer to my cup being not half full or half empty, but to being full as full can be. To speak of the wonderful is not to merely describe a situation as being pleasant or pleasing to the eyes – to be full of wonder is to express a sentiment regarding an experience that often cannot be explicitly described.

By wonder I do not mean, for my purposes here, to include the notion of an inquisitive spirit. To wonder is not to merely ask questions. A serious question regarding this or that may fall within the experience of one who wonders, but to isolate it merely in this context is misleading. The sentiment of what I am not considering can be captured in these simple phrases: I wonder if it will rain tonight? I wonder if I can? These statements can be restructured in the following ways: Will it rain tonight? Can I do it? The wonder I am after has little, if anything, to do with questions of this kind.

> I came on my first Military orchid, a species I had long wanted to encounter but hitherto had never seen outside a book. I fell on my knees before it in a way that all botanists will know, I identified…I measured, I photographed, I worked out where I was on the map, for future reference. I was excited, and very happy; one always remembers one's "firsts" of rare species. Yet five minutes after my wife had finally torn me away, I suffered a strange feeling. I realized that I had not actually seen the three plants in the little colony we had found…[3]

The honesty captured within this statement by John Fowles gives us an interesting look into an experience where the potential for wonder has been set aside. In short, it has been mediated and regulated by the desire to know and the desire to know now. The botanist's desire to "measure, photograph and to work" sets a very different tone than one who sits, who rests and who dwells. The irony is telling. By the very act of trying to comprehend and mechanically capture the flower, he missed apprehending and truly experiencing the flower in all of its apparent wonder. Fowles may wonder about the flower, but he does not dwell within and around the flower. To wonder is to experience the world in a way that must precede all forms of questioning. It is a phenomenological apprehension of what is presented to the senses. To wonder is to sit, to rest and to dwell.

A magician approaches. Sitting in the palm of her left hand is a large silver coin. It quickly reminds you of a poker chip, of cards, then gambling. For a moment you wonder if she is going to give you the coin. In what appears to be no more than a second or two you decide that the coin is not for you. There is no reason to question your surroundings. A coin is simply held in a hand. You are witnessing an ordinary and everyday experience. It is 12:30 pm on a Tuesday afternoon. You see a coin in the palm of a hand. Nothing about this moment is unique and nothing needs to be reflected upon or questioned. You do not notice the coin by noticing the coin. Your focus is unfocused. You are surrounded by your surroundings. You are at ease with their ordinariness. It is apart of your "average everydayness" and there is no reason for suspicion. There is a complacent "ready-to-hand" aspect to this experience that makes room for the experience. With deliberation the person takes the coin in their right fingertips and methodically displays it. Suspicion arises. You are now aware of your position in relation to the position of the coin. For reasons not yet known, you have slipped out of your ordinary experience and recognize this moment as different from the one that preceded it. The coin is held up towards you and it points in your direction. You notice the grip. You notice the coin.

And then you focus on what appears to be a proceeding of one sort or another. And proceed it does. This is no longer an average, everyday event. Expectations are imposed. In a moment a natural and ordinary experience has been formalized. You are suddenly aware of the person, the hand, the coin and a change in the posture of the other. At this point there is no occasion for an arousal of wonder. The coin is placed back into their left hand and their fingers curl into a closed fist around it. The coin is now out of sight. Your suspicion begins to grow. You have questions. For the time being, however, your suspicions and concerns are nothing more than unformulated and guarded questions. Slowly the fingers of the magician's left hand are opened. The coin is no longer there. It has, according to your immediate senses, vanished. You react with an incredulous, cautious and light gasp. Your surprise and astonishment lead to a simple, emotional response. You dwell. You dwell in wonder. And you are captured in the moment, by the moment and yet only for a moment. The coin has been displayed. It has vanished. Everything you have just experienced contradicts your previous understanding of how the world works. Objects do not just vanish. Immediately you demand an explanation. Your senses are clearly suspect as a Cartesian, empirical model imposes on the immediacy of your sensible concern. Your tone, body language and posture assume a new and offensive position. In an instant you experience a radical phenomenological shift and you move from a position of wonder to that of the wonderer. Like Descartes in the *Discourse* you choose a different path in the forest. Instead of wandering aimlessly, guided by your senses, you will take the rational and the reasonable path towards knowledge. The fork in the path pulls you towards a reconciliation of a particular sort. The wonder of the moment becomes a rational road hazard. An epistemological tree has fallen across the path of your experience. You have been jarred by your sense of reason. You have been thrown out of the experience. You question your senses. Instead of dwelling in the wonder of the moment, you wonder where the coin went. The experience has been rationally mediated.

Early on in the *Discourse* we read of a young Descartes who was interested in removing himself from his schooling as soon as possible so as to journey out into the world and see it for himself. He was interested in learning more. Knowledge for Descartes was the foundation. With knowledge came a certain type of under-standing that would allow for a wiser, fuller and sometimes more virtuous worldly approach.[4] As he tells the reader how he moved from student to teacher, he speaks about the world in what I will call a wonder full way.[5] His love for books is evident. He viewed reading as a way into other people's minds. Based on my earlier def-inition, it seems to me that Descartes recognized the wonder sur-rounding this kind of personal, literal and historical access. There was an element of surprise at play here. This was something to be marveled at. He acknowledged that reading was an opportunity to dialogue with others past and present. He refers to the ability of the reader to step out beyond her scope and outside of her perspective precisely because of access to so many different writers. Is it not fair to say that this is a wonder full approach to reading, writing and the Other?[6] The objects of Descartes' attention here are not important; however, his experience is.

Ironically, Descartes writes that he wanted to leave his studies behind and pursue the "great book of the world."[7] Perhaps he had had enough. Perhaps he had turned one too many pages in this great and vast worldly text. It was time to move on. He suggests that travelling through other ideas and cultures would enable him to function with a greater capacity for understanding. It seems to me that Descartes was captured by wonder. His willingness to be open to possibilities that did not reflect his own seems to imply a sense of dwelling. In other words, he was open to the wonder and the surprise that his experience might create. He may have been looking for certainty, but he wasn't afraid of or intimidated by another perspective. However, the *Discourse* tells us that this approach lasted for approximately nine years.[8] It was after his studying, reading and travelling that he started to put pen to paper and record his method for all things scientific. His primary focus had shifted. His method had been established. Mathematics was his guide and exactitude his goal. He was committed to the framework. Geometry was a premise, the sum his conclusion. He wanted answers. His experience of dwelling in wonder had been mediated by a rational reconciliation of the mind. He had accepted the framework and his assumptions were well beyond the preliminary stages of wonder. The wonder, the questions and the inquiry had been addressed as far as he was concerned. He now attempted to record his observations as fact. The passions were to be approached in a mathematical and deductive way. Wonder was to be regulated within a methodological and seemingly scientific framework. Descartes was done with wonder.

Early in the *Passions* he writes about how to determine what the passions are and how they function in relation to the body and the soul. He gets very specific in his explanation. He speaks of the movement of muscles and the heart; he tells us that the animal spirits are the cause of the body's passionate response; he writes about the lungs filling with fluid as a result of the passions' effect on the body.[9] What is of interest to us here are the assumptions made about the passions. Descartes wanted to regulate the passions. He wanted to bring them under control. In short, he was looking to rationally mediate all things excessively wonder full. Descartes was more interested in the mechanics behind the passions than the experience of the passions themselves.

According to Descartes, wonder is the stepping-stone to the soul. It is the genesis for the other passions to grow out of.[10] Descartes sought the first cause of this passion. He wanted to benefit from the soul's understanding of these "primitive" experiences. He was looking to extract utility out of the passions and out of the body in order to accommodate and enhance the nature and function of the soul. Wonder was important for the soul's development, but too much wonder was considered harmful. He writes of it in terms of excess and defect – an Aristotelian notion of moral and ethical imbalance. Too much was seen as an impediment to the rational side and it was Descartes' desire that the individual rid themselves of any excess of this passion. He writes that wonder is useful for the sciences and that it can "entirely eradicate or pervert the use of reason" and that to "prevent excessive wonder there is no remedy but to acquire knowledge of many things."[11] Knowledge becomes the controlling mechanism within the experience of wonder. Is it possible that reason and rationality drive a wedge between the body's experience of wonder and the soul's ability to file, manage and use wonder as a bridge to a clearer understanding of the truth of and in our experience?

Acquiring knowledge, then, is pursued for the sake of knowledge. To know more is to know. To know more is to know less about the phenomenology of experience and to know more about what informs that experience. Is it not fair to say that pursuing the answer with only a utilitarian goal in mind is a misunderstanding and misapprehension of the subtle nuances of the particular and varied constituents of our combined experience? If an experience of wonder is viewed as a potential for Aristotelian moral excess, wonder is viewed as a temporary means and knowledge the end. I have been successful and now I know, and will no longer, for the moment and within this moment, wonder. I will effectively monitor and deal with this Cartesian notion of moral, phenomenological decay. The rational transaction will be complete. Wonder will be pushed out, moved aside and painted over in lieu of the pending answer and solution. The magician vanishes the coin and the spectator observes and wonders. However, it seems to me that the experience itself is momentary at best as the desire to know overtakes and mediates. The spectator does not dwell in wonder. On the contrary they observe, they wonder, they explain. And like Descartes, they too are done with wonder.

An insatiable desire to know drives a rationalistic wedge between the experience of the wonderer and the wonder itself. The background of wonder is blurred by the foreground of potential epistemic achievement. There is no need to dwell in wonder. Wonder becomes an evidential step towards a definitive empirical resolution. In short, knowledge is the panacea to all things excessively wonderful. Knowledge satisfies, quenches and regulates the thirst that wonder may create. Wonder succumbs to a form of Cartesian rational mediation. Wonder may be a catalyst for knowledge within this mechanistic model, but it is assigned an inferior phenomenological role as mind and matter take precedence. Like the child who no longer finds comfort in the simple act of playing, we are hypnotized by the primacy of reason. Childhood's innocence is stained by an adolescent rational maturity. And like the adolescent who leaves the world of make-believe and play behind her, we flee from the wonder and find comfort and rest in the rational. We become mature, philosophical grown-ups.

Good philosophy may begin in wonder, but it does not necessarily stay there; nor am I suggesting that it should. However, what is the rush? Why must philosophy move out beyond the wonder full and conquer it in such a regimented and effectual manner? Why not build, dwell and think within wonder? What is it that drives this necessity to know and to know more now? For if we scratch that epistemological itch, wonder recedes. It is no longer a part of our environment, but is experienced, interpreted and situated within a rational and Cartesian universe. Everyday, average experience can induce feelings of wonder. We are surrounded by experiential gold mines of wonder full potential. To answer directly is to know more now than a moment ago. The difference between the now and the not yet may be measured by all things wonder full. The rich complexity of our everyday experience is begging us to dwell – and dwell we must. To dwell in wonder is to know less now, but to know wonder more.

EIGHT

RETIRED HUMANS

"You have to begin to lose your memory, if only in bits and pieces, to realize that memory is what makes our lives. Life without memory is no life at all...our memory is our coherence, our reason, our feeling, even our action. Without it, we are nothing..." —Luis Bunuel

Consider for a moment the notion of your own past relational experience. One by one, remove the memories of all your interactions with friends, family and personally significant acquaintances. Slowly you are reduced to something else – something other than you are as you exist today. Past experiences and memories of those experiences situate you within the present, explain the past and help to formulate the path you may take in the future. Without these traces of your past to use as self-referential points of authentic identification, you are in effect lost – without direction, wandering through a forest with no map or guide to tell you where you have previously travelled. No trail has been blazed, and your footsteps are impossible to retrace. You are essentially a different person, paralyzed, situated somewhere between the past and a misunderstood present. You may be able to think of the past, imagine a past, but it is not *your* past. If what preceded your present is ultimately responsible for who you are today, then an inability to remember would undermine your notion of self and authenticity, and in so doing it would compromise your humanity.

Oliver Sacks in *The Man Who Mistook His Wife for a Hat* tells the story of the "Lost Mariner," a man who has virtually no recollection beyond 1945. His short-term memory has been compromised as a result of what appears to be a neurological disorder or perhaps a wartime experience. Unable to reminisce, he is left in the unenviable position of a self without a previous and complex set of experiential reference points. "Jimmie both was and wasn't aware of this deep, tragic loss in himself, loss of himself. If a man loses a leg or an eye, he knows he has lost a leg or an eye; but if he has lost a self – himself – he cannot know it, because he is no longer there to know it."[1]

Blade Runner's recent appearance in updated two-disc, four-disc and five-disc DVD versions is an indication of the film's presence and power twenty-five years after its initial release. It is a visionary, visual spectacle and one of my favourite films. Although it is a futuristic science fiction piece, on closer examination we see a meaningful revelation of very current human and existential concerns. Each viewing brings a fuller and richer understanding of what it means to be *living* in the world.

Blade Runner,[2] Ridley Scott's adaptation of Philip K. Dick's novel *Do Androids Dream of Electric Sheep?* is a film about authenticity.[3] It portrays a bleak and dystopic future in which the nonreal competes with and overtakes the real. As Scott Bukatman reminds us, "The ultimate relevance of *Blade Runner* lies in its doubled, complex understanding of what it must mean to be human… [I]n a postmodern world of mass media, spectacle and simulation, it becomes increasingly difficult to tell the difference between humans and replicants."[4] The narrative format of the film dialectically pits the authentic against the inauthentic, the human against the replicant and the simulation against the self. It is a reminder that simulation is a comprehensive form of manipulation.[5] The often thin line between reality and hyperreality has not only moved, but has become increasingly blurred and even difficult to define. In short, *Blade Runner* is a visual portrayal of our world in deep self-referential crisis.

Blade Runner sheds significant light on personhood, the self[6] and human authenticity, without providing clear answers to the philosophical and psychological human dilemma it portrays. Through its visual layout, narrative structure and technical approach, this film constitutes an essay on the self and the various aspects that make up the self. Its dystopic[7] tone supports the notion that we in the West are in deep existential doubt about the self. "Dystopias generally project into the future the fears of the present, and their themes often transcode the sorts of anxieties that characterized that crisis – uncontrolled corporations, untrustworthy leaders, a breakdown of legitimacy, rising crime, etc."[8]

Memory – the capacity to remember in a dynamic and authentic manner – is a powerful theme throughout the film. The film asks these questions: Who are we without a personal file of memorable past experiences that we can access implicitly and explicitly? Without such a file, do we or can we have an authentic version or vision of ourselves?

In a similar way, the replicants of *Blade Runner,* manufactured and thrust ready-made into the present, are faced with the question of what it means to be a self or even to have the notion of a self. Where there is no way to authenticate one's former self, the very notion of selfhood is in question and may not hold up under scrutiny. Without a dynamic recollection of a former self or self-knowledge (whether explicit or implicit), the self cannot have a relevant existence in the present. It may be human, but its selfhood is in question. The replicants of *Blade Runner* clearly feel and understand this negation of experience and loss of the narrative and historical self.

The city of Los Angeles of 2019 is a city that contributes to this loss by negating individuality. It has been constructed with the corporation in mind, with profit and efficiency as its primary goals, and it ideologically dwarfs and overpowers the individual's sense of self. Its panoptic gaze[9] reaches far and wide, so that the individual, awash in the corporate control and excess that characterize the city, easily loses any sense of self and human uniqueness, capitulating with almost no resistance. From the opening sequence of the film we are reminded of the dehumanizing effects of the vast cityscape: the individual is squashed by the spectacle, squashed beneath the buildings of corporate origin and the grandiose architectural decadence of the city's construction. In a tight close-up of the omnipresent eye we see a reflection of the postmodern steel-and-concrete puzzle, dark, ominous and foreboding, that constitutes the city. The eye looks out on a cold, dark and deeply depressing spectacle, and the film shouts, "Is this what we have become?"

As the film continues we are reminded literally and metaphorically of the infinitesimal size and insignificance of the human being in the shadow of the corporate giant of Los Angeles – suggesting, however subtly, that the present is not quite enough to anchor the self and give it meaning. This is a city whose business is to further an ideology of disconnection, detachment and normalization. Neville Wakefield states, "Everything in the city space speaks of a recycling process that denies linguistic, architectural or geographic specificities."[10] David Clarke suggests that this is in fact an "infernal reflection of an inhuman cityscape."[11] In the words of Gloria Pastorino, "One's position in society is measured by how high one's floor is in the city's vertiginous skyscrapers."[12] The entire *mise en scène* is dedicated to undermining what it means to be human, visually stimulating in the inhabitants and the viewer a sense of meaninglessness and personal irrelevance.

This sense of human insignificance is underscored by a later scene in which Deckard is picked up by Gaff and taken to see Bryant, the head of the police department's Blade Runner unit. We see Deckard and Gaff from an exterior shot in their space vehicle as it slowly moves up and out of the frame. This is followed by a quick cut to a computer terminal inside the ship, showing us the computer-generated image of their ascent. We are privy to the technical and visual specifics of their departure. The small speck on the screen graphically represents the tininess and insignificance of their vehicle, and this point is made again as the film cuts to an exterior shot in which the vehicle appears as a small light moving onward and upward into the expressionistic tunnel of the sky-scrapers above. We see small colored lights flashing ineffectually in a maze of concrete buildings beside and above them, reinforc-ing the idea that we are less than ourselves in this bewildering and overbearing ideological town. Like the landscape of the city, the foundation has been laid in the film from the beginning to suggest that the self is in crisis.

Having laid this visual foundation in terms of the story's setting, Scott's careful direction of the film heightens and extends our discomfort by raising the question of authenticity and blurring the line between the real and the synthetic aspects of the replicant and human. In several of the death sequences in the film, Deckard suffers great personal and emotional conflict as he kills or "retires" replicants. We viewers are emphatically situated within the narrative of the film and are asked by the filmmaker to put ourselves in the characters' shoes – to experience the relationship between the hunter and the hunted. We feel the turmoil of Deckard, but Scott clearly wishes us to empathize more deeply with the victims, in this case the replicants. Yet we are also prodded to question the source of this empathy; we must be constantly on our emotional guard and check our responses. For if the replicants are not authentically human, then what are they?

Deckard chases Zhora, his first "retirement" victim in the film, through the crowded streets. Via a series of handheld camera shots, fast cuts, tight facial close-ups and fast pans, we get a sense of the tension and fear Zhora is feeling as she flees for her life. In a sense, she foreshadows Batty's line later in the film, "I want more life," by running wildly through the streets in search of precisely that: more life. It is a response that is entirely human, or at least entirely that of a living being. And she seems to have legitimate reasons to want to go on living, reasons that have to do not so much with her implanted and synthetic past as with her recent knowledge of her real and memorable past: she has in some way learned what it means to be human, what it means to authentically remember. Clearly she has acquired experiences, memories and emotions that are crying out and encouraging her to "live."

These humanizing film techniques enhance and increase our ability to empathize with Zhora, and this in turn ironically casts an absurd light on the viewer. If this is a machine, then why am I feeling sorry for it? Why might I feel one way or another about something that has been manufactured merely for corporate profit? Even the use of the word "retire" in opposition to "kill" highlights this tension.

Deckard eventually fires on Zhora and is visibly shaken by the events that surround her poetic death – as are we. He has clear and deep personal misgivings about what he must do. The empathy and pathos we feel as viewers are extreme as we see Zhora propelled in slow motion through broken glass and windows. She falls and slowly gets up, fighting for more life. The camera allows us to view the intimate details of her death: the exit holes of Deckard's bullets are large, bloody and severe. We are meant to interact emotionally with the replicant; we are prompted to feel sorry for something that we know is a simulation. The slow-motion technique, backed by the operatic and romantic music of Vangelis, heightens the intensity and horror of this sequence. As Zhora dies we hear faintly in the background the sound of a heartbeat. Again the question is effectively raised – human or replicant?

Deckard's own ambivalence influences us. After Deckard retires her, we see him purchasing some alcohol to assuage the guilt and anxiety that follow. Obviously, he feels the same tension that we feel about Zhora's authenticity as a human. Scott invites us as voyeurs to relate both with Deckard, who seems to have experienced the event as a killing, and with Zhora – and later on her replicated teammates. "It is...a question of substituting signs of the real for the real itself...[S]imulation threatens the difference between 'true' and 'false,' between 'real' and 'imaginary,'" writes Jean Baudrillard.[13] The philosophical tone of the film's narrative encourages the viewer to ask deeper and more penetrating questions about the notion of self.

Memory is held up as one of the clearest ways of delineating between the self and the virtual self in *Blade Runner*. The Tyrell Corporation is in the business of manufacturing genetic creations. These are in fact simulations, attempts to create something that has all the characteristics of a human and at the same time is not human. The corporate logo and mandate, "More human than human," is Tyrell's attempt at commercial omniscience. He has become the arrogant and egocentric creator. Even the implanted, generic, simulated past given to replicants is a form of corporate control. As Tyrell himself tells us:

> We begin to see in them a strange obsession. After all, they are emotionally inexperienced, with only a few short years in which to store up the experiences you and I take for granted. If we gift them with a past we create a cushion or a pillow for their emotions and consequently we can control them better.[14]

But although the replicants have developed emotions, they have no definitive past. "Did you get your precious photographs?" asks Roy Batty of Leon, a "friend" and fellow replicant, implying and reinforcing the notion that photographs are a key to the past. The replicant is concerned about losing his "precious" photos and with them his only link to that which is primarily a human interaction with the past: memory. In fact, for all replicants, photographs are the only link to a past they never actually had. What are the implications of this dilemma? Are photographs synonymous with the past? Can they be equated to memory? Or are they merely mechanical representations of former events and therefore only virtual signifiers of what may or may not have come before? If I have a photo of myself doing something that I do not ever remember taking part in, can I legitimately say that this recorded event is actually part of who I am? Am I now referring to a real self or a fabricated self? To quote Annette Kuhn:

> The family photographs produced by the replicant Rachel in *Blade Runner* as "proof" that she is human likewise appeals to the slender promise of real-world referentiality embodied in the

photo as a chemically produced image; and yet this promise also calls into question whatever confidence we might have in the truth of the memories that we read off our photographs.[15]

Clearly, Rachel and Leon are concerned with losing the link to what they believe is their unique and individual past. They have been taught, or programmed to believe, that there is significant ideological power to the photograph and its contents. Rachel, for example, believes that the photo she carries with her is the sign and reminder of her humanity. It is not only a connection to her past, it has become her past. It is a mechanical and virtual representation of what never was, and yet she believes, however precariously, that this mechanical record *is* part of her self, that this *was* her self as a child. It is, for her, simple proof of her childhood and therefore of her identity as a living human organism. It is this historical evidence that allows her to make claims about an authentic present and former self. The photograph of her standing *virtually* with her mother clearly brings her emotional comfort.

When Deckard raises a question about the authenticity of her past, therefore, Rachel is visibly upset and shaken by the obvious implications. He tells her that the memories she has of playing doctor as a child and of watching spiders hatch, are probably implants of someone else's memories. Deckard confirms her suspicions about her own identity, and her questions begin. "Not only is the photograph never, in essence, a memory, but it actually blocks memory, quickly, and quickly becomes a counter-memory," writes Roland Barthes in his work on photography.[16] Barthes insists that the photograph is not synonymous with memory; it is at best a catalyst for memory. And in Rachel and Leon's case it is neither catalyst nor memory, but entirely simulation. The simulation replaces the real. Without authentic memories of the past, without a frame of reference to account for its existence, the self is left reeling in a nonreferential state somewhere between the real and the nonreal.

Emotion is potentially another "sign" of authentic humanity. Replicants in Scott's world have developed emotions, and they clearly feel. Pain and fear seem to be driving them forward in their search for more life. They have lived long enough and retained enough experience to know what it feels like to love and to hate. Pris and Roy have developed a relationship that is clearly based on human relational reference points; Deckard and Rachel are falling in love and are doing things that humans who love one another do; Leon understands what it is like to live in fear. But does their experience of emotion mean that these replicants have an authentic understanding of themselves? Without a real past, are they capable of making self-referential and ultimately authentic claims?

In one of the final and pivotal scenes of the film, Roy Batty dies. It is a peaceful, convincingly human death. Batty has saved Deckard's life. He seems to be at ease with his impending death, and as he dies we sense a level of connection between the two characters that was not evident until this point. Deckard empathizes with Roy, clearly touched by the experience of seeing him die, and the audience is asked to do the same. We see Deckard's face in a tight close-up as he closes his eyes momentarily as if to pray for Roy and reflect on this "man's" death. Roy's final words re-emphasize the tension between the real and the nonreal. Roy has acted, experienced and felt; he has for all practical purposes lived a human life. From a wider-angled shot we see him kneeling on the rooftop, dying in the rain, and with a large, lighted TDK billboard in the background we listen to his last words: "I have seen things you people wouldn't believe...all those moments will be lost in time like tears in the rain." Roy has seen and he remembers, and those memories, those moments unique to him, will be lost. With an advertisement for a company in the business of mechanical reproduction as his backdrop, Roy dies.

A powerful sense of loss is communicated at this point in the film. Again we are in the difficult position of feeling sad and sorry for a machine. A shot of the remorseful Deckard dissolves slowly into a close-up of Roy's dead and peaceful face, once again blurring the line between the reality and the simulation and raising the question of humanity and authenticity.

I am not suggesting that to be authentically human one needs *only* an active and reliable memory. What I am proposing is that without memory we have no reference for who we are as individuals and what the self may or may not include. Without a past and without a history, for instance, would I be a Canadian? I would physically exist, but how would I or anyone else know whether or not I was of Canadian descent? I need a story. I need a past. To ensure a meaningful and relevant present I need a memorable connection with all that has preceded this moment in time. Authenticity is connected not only to who we are, but more fundamentally to who we have been.

What do these questions have to say about how I approach my past, about how I interact with what has come before? The notion of false memory is something we have encountered in our culture. How does one appropriately address these types of concerns? In an interview before his death, Philip K. Dick identified the two topics that fascinated him most and that he wanted to write about all the time: "What is reality?" and "What constitutes the authentic human being?"[17]

The problem that the replicants, like the postmodern subject, have to confront, is how to produce themselves and give substantiality to their lives when history and in particular the means of self-historising, documenting or narrating the self have lost any 'real' credibility – when they too take on the depthlessness of simulation.[18]

In the initial Voight-Kampff[19] sequence in the film, Deckard comes to realize that Rachel is not human. We are aware of the line between simulation and reality and we watch it blur out of focus. "She's a replicant," says Deckard to Tyrell. "How can it not know what it is?" In the same sentence Deckard refers to her as both "she" and "it." He too is confused: human or machine? It is also interesting to note that in most of the scenes where we see Rachel and Deckard interact, it is Rachel who seems to exude the confidence that ought to characterize real persons. She is comfortable with who she is, and seems to understand Deckard in a way that perhaps even he can't see. Her questions and her presence suggest that she is in control. In the first elevator sequence in the film we see Deckard enter what appears to be an empty elevator. The camera is careful to suggest that he is alone. However, once inside we view the scene from another perspective, which turns out to be Rachel's. Once Deckard realizes he is not alone, he pulls his gun and reacts frantically in fear and panic. Then the camera cuts to Rachel in the corner, looking calm, cool and very collected; she understands his fear and concern as she takes control with her serene presence. She is, in effect, authoritative and self-aware, while the human, Deckard, is bereft of presence of mind and acting reflexively. The replicant is, for the time being, behaving as a human and to borrow a phrase from the film, "more human than human." As Bukatman points out, "The underlying issue is not whether we can give a machine the qualities of the human, but whether the human has lost its humanity; whether it has become, in fact, a machine."[20]

Questions regarding the self are intertwined with questions concerning simulation, historicity and authenticity. If the distinction between the real and the nonreal continues to atrophy into a dystopic blur, how can one clearly know when the obliterated line has been crossed?

NINE

LIFE'S ONLY CONSTANT

"Buddhism promises nothing but actually fulfills; Christianity promises everything, but fulfills nothing." —Nietzsche

Whether we acknowledge it or not, we are agents of change. What we do affects the environment and others around us. Like giants walking through a miniature town, we are often oblivious to the effects of our actions. But each one of us can have a profound, positive effect on the world. Consider a line of dominos. When one tile is removed from the line, the chain of toppling tiles is broken. The momentum grinds to a halt. One minor adjustment to the line results in a major change. Individual acts do matter.

I grew up in the Christian church and for better or worse the relationship has not always been a healthy one for me. I have high expectations of a group that claims to have access to the truth. So when it says one thing and does another I get upset.

Recently I've come to view the church as a not-so-sophisticated social club. Members meet at regularly prescribed intervals to gather and gab, chatting briefly about what's happening in their busy lives. We listen as someone preaches, tuning out if the sermon goes too long, and then we leave to get back to our hectic schedules. But aren't we missing the point? It's true that our lives, families and work matter, and that our issues need to be addressed; but what about the Other we are called to be mindful of? In accepting that individual choices can make a difference in the world, we begin to see that we cannot be satisfied with the status quo. Evil must not triumph.

To be fair, the church has had a positive impact in the world in times past. Plenty of relief and development organizations have faith-based roots, and the church has done a remarkable job in many arenas of social change and influence. But too often the good works are forgotten as gossip of its weaknesses and shortcomings spreads. The cynic in us says a single vote or a single bottle of water doesn't matter, while scoffing headlines uncover egomaniacal tele-visual prophets who work with over-indulgent budgets, melodra-matic theatrics, dated image consultants and bad hairdressers.

At times like this, it's helpful to remember that we are a part of a tradition that has often been on the cutting edge of social issues. Think Dietrich Bonhoeffer, William Wilberforce, Mother Teresa, the Good Samaritan or Martin Luther. Think salt and light. Are we still affecting significant change, or are we following behind others as they march and beat the drum for social justice?

Choosing to care about our neighbours is a moral obligation insofar as we redefine what it means to be human and to the extent that we allow our humanity to affect everything we do. We don't need any more reasons to think about ourselves. We have perfected that.

All of us need to be shocked out of our complacency. Discovering other layers to the onion that is our worldview can be invigorating and exciting. On the other hand, it can also be unsettling and quite disturbing. Consider the story Jesus told about the rich young ruler. This young leader wanted to know from his teacher what he had to do to inherit eternal life. Christ told him he had to sell everything he owned and come and follow him. The rich young man had questions and yet he wasn't prepared for his teacher's response. His question was risky, but that's where his faith began and ended. He talked action yet lived inaction. The truth of the matter, or any matter, is often unsettling. I can only imagine how this privileged young leader reacted. Disappointed and disillusioned with his comfortable, hypocritical lifestyle, he silently walked away.

Too often wealth, status and celebrity subvert a socially just and relevant heart. In the *Pensées* Pascal wrote: "Man's sensitivity to the littlest things and insensitivity to the greatest things are marks of a very strange disorder." Has evil triumphed around the world because we spend a little too much time grooming, buying and scrambling for success of one kind or another? Are we walking along the road less travelled or are we merely travelling the road less and less?

Love must change everything. Action over inaction. Graceful choice over complacency. Loving others and all it encompasses is our call to change. Believe it. Bear it and hope for it. The life of the soul must be radical love. Social and cultural transformation depends on a global movement that realizes its privileged capacity and the influence it both has had and can have.

Change is imminent. Change is on the horizon. We are the dominoes. We are falling gracefully, and we must trust in a long line of historical renewal that will not leave others behind.

Inshallah.

TEN

WHITE, WESTERN AND WAIST-DEEP

"When the missionaries came to Africa they had the Bible and we had the land. They said 'Let us pray.' We closed our eyes. When we opened them we had the Bible and they had the land."
—Desmond Tutu

I stepped out of the small wooden boat as we aligned ourselves along the Mekong river's edge. It had been raining the last few days, and yet I was still unprepared for the muddy hill that met me as I climbed out of the canoe-like craft. I had managed to escape the swarm of red fire ants that were circling around my body in the bottom of the boat as I anticipated our arrival. Believe me, these little critters bite. And they bite hard. Size doesn't matter when it comes to fire ants. An entomological force to be reckoned with – six tiny legs and powerful little jaws. Thankfully I avoided the flesh-eating frenzy.

As I tripped my way to the top of the steep riverbank I stood up, taking care not to slide back down the muddy slope. The first thing I noticed was a rusty well-pump handle not three metres away. I moved closer. I pushed back the jungle brush to see if the pump was working. It wasn't. In bold rusty letters the name of the NGO was branded on its side, along with the installation date, 1999. As we travelled throughout the community, we found rusty wells littered here and there. It was clear that those who funded the water project would not be as proud of their wells now as they were the day after drilling down into the jungle water table. Same NGO. Same problem. The wells hadn't been used in years. With a ghost town feel to them, they were a perfect example of a shoddy needs assessment. Had the development team asked a few more questions perhaps these wells would still be in use today. As a philosopher I have always been more interested in the questions. Answers often leave little room for creative growth and development. They can easily shut down the conversation, and for me the conversation is what it's all about. The dialogue. However, keeping all this in mind, what exactly is a good needs assessment? Answers assume so much.

As the day passed us by, we visited families throughout the area. I played some pool in the middle of the jungle on a worn out and warped table protected from the elements by some bamboo. I lost the game. Snookered, actually. I even got involved in a local game of chance. A few men were having a great time gambling away a little money on what appeared to be a dice game of a particular sort. They let me in. It is wonderful and powerful memories like these that help us to cross cultural boundaries, but they are almost always full of simple life-changing lessons to be learned.

It wasn't till later that afternoon that I came upon my first Bio-Sand Water Filter (BSF) – a remarkable Canadian invention which was in full use at the only rural maternity clinic in the area. Dirty water is poured into the top of the filter and trickles down to result in a fresh cup of water dripping out of the tap below. The rusty well pumps were rusty not because of a poor needs assessment, or because the community lost interest, or because of insufficient community-based training. They were rusty because of arsenice and disuse. Who could have known that industry situated on the Mekong a thousand miles away would compromise the water supply of this quiet Cambodian community? A polluted water table. A deadly chemical hard to taste and impossible to see. And so the wells rusted away. I couldn't help but wonder if the poisonous chemical would have taken the rust clean off the now useless pumps.

In *King Leopold's Ghost*, his marvellous book about the slave trade, the exploitation of the Congo and the Belgian rubber industry, Adam Hochschild writes about how most of the written historical records we have of this particular period in the Congo's history are perspectives of white eyes. Without a doubt this is problematic on many levels. Hochschild writes, "At first, Africans apparently saw the white sailors not as men but as vumbi – ancestral ghosts – since the Kongo people believed that a person's skin changed to the color of chalk when he passed into the land of the dead."[1] I trust we are not all passing through the land of the dead, but if this sentiment is true, and I believe it is on many levels, it is instructive for us now to think about how we can avoid this kind of tragic misunderstanding in the future. History is instructive for so many reasons.

Standing at over six feet and lacking any definite tone to my skin colour, I am often seen as the white, Western male when I come to a project. By white and Western I mean I can be viewed as the rich man with the answers, experience, backing of large international organizations and so on. This is a pigeonhole that is hard to escape. I don't want to be looked at as the one with all of the solutions, or with any of the solutions, for that matter. I want to be a partner. What does it mean to partner and how does one play it out in a development context in a meaningful manner? Mary Anderson reminds us that we are to do no harm.[2] How does the big white guy with plenty of schooling, lots of varied experiences and good intentions steer clear of making things worse? How do I avoid doing damage of various sorts? Good intentions are without a doubt not enough. Healthy approaches to development require the ability to stand back and say that I may have been wrong. Too often my ego precedes me.

One of my favourite pictures in my collection was taken in Cambodia in 2004. My wife, Elizabeth, and I were on a house building trip together. Working alongside a local NGO, we managed to help construct about ten small homes on stilts in a community about forty-five minutes outside Phnom Penh. That's where I met Sok. He's a carpenter. In the photo you can see I'm standing beside – towering over, actually – this friend and colleague doing excellent groundwork there. We shared some Coke and conversation together. Note the fanny pack around his waist. That's what I was using to carry my nails in for the project. It saved me a lot of time moving up and down the ladder to get more nails. It was a simple lesson in time management and cost me two US dollars in the Russian market. Probably more than what Sok was making at the time for several days' wages. The notion of extreme poverty can be somewhat meaningless until you meet people like Sok. I gave him the pack. I trust he is still using it or something like it today.

This picture captures, for me, where meaningful connection happens in international development. It's in the individual relationships we build – being colleagues, co-workers, partners and, dare I say it, friends. It is through these relationships that our work in the field gains traction and moves forward. Ian Smillie reminds us that we are indeed partners. Capacity building must be about coming alongside and knowing when to leave, get out and move on.

> Even in deliberate, developmental capacity building projects, there are problems in knowing how to approach the issue, how to measure, and how to evaluate it...training is not a panacea... it is not in any way synonymous with capacity building...And a general lesson about capacity building, one now decades old, is that builders must have good knowledge of "buildees." Their society, and the context in which the effort is expected to take place.[3]

We've all heard it said that it's all about relationships. Too often development is driven by the bottom line and "quantifiable" things like results-based management. But where do you situate the sanctity of human life within such numbers? You can't build relationships on a pie chart or a graph. Instead, they are built on love and respect for the Other. Holistic, meaningful growth requires that relationships be grounded in trust and rooted in passionate intentions. If you can't start here, then sustainable development is doomed.

We all know that relationships matter. And that they require a deliberate investment of time and effort. Sometimes, though, I wonder how well we have apprehended the idea that they also demand a little heart and a whole lot of soul. Holistic development must be situated within the heartfelt practices of listening well and acting intentionally. Lend a hand, but first lean in and lend your ear to the conversation. We must be available. We must be aware. And we must act. A spirit of partnership has always been the basis for all meaningful relationships. They are ends in themselves. Believe and build. This is the future of our field.

On my most recent trip to Cambodia I saw very little sun. The country experienced more rain than they had in the past fifteen years or so. There was serious flooding everywhere. One day the airport had to be closed down as the runway vanished below the rising waters. It's a good reminder for me of the impact we can have as development workers. It is a lesson for me once again in humility and respect. At points I found myself wading through waist-deep water, not knowing where to step. It was indeed a metaphor for not knowing what's next. I see it as a good reminder that international development work is a difficult road to travel, one that needs constant refining, good questions, consistency, clarity and a whole lot of passion.

Waist-deep, we press on.

ELEVEN

NETWORKING 101

"Man is a knot into which relationships are tied."
—Antoine de Saint-Exupéry

Networking to my students is a bad word and something they would rather not think about. Often misunderstood and rarely practised well, it is something you can only learn by doing. One needs to work out the latent relational skills we all have picked up somewhere along the way. Networking is about relationships, and relationships take time to water, nurture, develop and build.

Simply put, networking is about making connections, building relationships and harnessing trust.

Think of a large river with tributaries. It's all connected. We're all linked in one way or another. Some call it the *six degrees of separation*. Look up the phrase on the Internet and you'll be amazed.

It means, in short, that a very small number of people are linked to everyone else in a few simple steps and that the rest of us are linked to the world through those special few.

Networking takes time. Be enthusiastic. Let your passion flow. Be intentional and view every handshake as important. It's essential. Sincerity is key to making all of this work. If you view others merely as means to an end, in this case you are in trouble. People can sniff out insincerity and disingenuous behaviour. Make eye contact and assume very little. Give yourself a reason to follow up. Get their business card and you are on your way to creating a network of committed people. These people give us access to worlds and opportunities to which we wouldn't normally have access to.

Here are six simple principles I use as a guide.

1. Make the call. Make contact. Make the first move.
2. Ask good questions
3. Go the extra mile
4. Give before you take
5. Do what you say and always follow through
6. Apologize if necessary

Working in international development requires a keen ability to network, build new relationships and connect the relational dots. Continue to meet people in all related fields that share similar interests, passions and goals. What is the downside?

I remember interviewing an American entertainer for an article I was writing. When we finished I promised to send along a copy of the interview unedited on CD as a small thank you. The individual thanked me and the ninety-minute phone call came to an end. Two days later I sent the interview via registered mail. He received it within two days and immediately called me back. "David, thank you. I've done hundreds of interviews over the years and you are the only person who has ever followed through and sent me a copy for my archives." I was stunned. Astounding, I thought, that I was the first and only one to do what I said I would do. Following through meant committing to something I promised. Not that hard to do, really, but apparently not always practised.

If you want to begin networking, start today. Commit. Exhibit a passionate heart. Be yourself and the connections will come.

TWELVE

EVERY BEAN YOU GRIND

"Transformative social change happens at the intersection of compassion and enlightened self-interest." —Paul Collier

Coffee that has been freshly ground always smells better than it tastes. And I think it tastes pretty good. Life's like that sometimes – full of visual and olfactory delights, yet on some level a bit of a disappointment. You expect one thing and often wind up with another.

I take my coffee with double cream and one sugar. I like it strong, but not too strong. I was sipping a fairly hefty, dark-roasted bean one Saturday morning, reflecting on the power of the individual and the cumulative impact of little things, when I saw a coin on the floor. I wondered how many loose pennies might be piling up in coffee cans and shoeboxes around the world. I imagined a lot of money – a mountain of pennies, a sea of copper idly waiting for a reason to re-engage and get back into the fiscal game. Then I unearthed an astounding statistic: there are over $2 billion worth of pennies sitting around people's homes, garages and piggy banks throughout the US! Two billion dollars! Do the math: that's a lot of pennies. My old analog calculator can't handle numbers that big, and neither can I. All I know is, that's a lot of money collecting dust, money that could be used for valuable and critical things like clean drinking water, medical research, TB shots, ARVs and food – the list is as long as the mountain of pennies is high. One penny at a time adds up to a significant amount of cold, hard cash. It is collective wealth in limbo, waiting. Every penny, every thought, every kind act and every coffee bean is part of a much larger whole.

Like the collective wealth lying around the US in stagnant copper, the fair trade coffee industry is growing. It currently represents one percent of the world's coffee trade and is effecting change one bean at a time. Coffee is the second most traded product around the world. With a rate of consumption of over twelve billion pounds a year, it is also one of the most exploited. When I think of the amount of money I have spent on coffee at a rate of two or three cups a day, I shudder at the impact. How many beans have I consumed? What effect have I had on the environment and on the farmer who is overworked and underpaid? Every time I enjoy my early morning caffeine injection, I am potentially contributing to exploitation of the most significant kind. At two cups of coffee a day, I will consume an annual harvest of eighteen coffee trees. That's a lot of beans. The exponential potential is huge.

According to Fairtrade Canada, small family farmers grow over fifty percent of the world's coffee. Working with fair trade practices, these coffee farmers are able to earn three to five times more than they would by selling their beans through local middlemen. International standards have been set that guarantee a minimum price is paid directly to co-ops and farmers. Alexa Marin Colindres, a member of Prodecoop from Nicaragua, reported:

With fair trade income we have made improvements to our community. Before, we slept on the ground and did not have basic amenities. Now some of us have floors, some furniture, sanitary services, and potable water. If we sold all of our production at Fair Trade prices, our dreams would come true.[1]

One person, one family, one bean at time.

Farmer-owned organizations are acting together to produce quality beans that are organic (that is, produced without the use of agrochemicals) and shade-grown. But these organizations are not only environmentally sound; they are also concerned about the social capital of their investments. Fair trade has been responsible for improved access to low-interest loans, improved social services, more sophisticated technology and communication systems, transportation equipment and infrastructure, and technical training and skills diversification. By employing a sustainable and restorative approach, these farmers will create agreeable economic and social relationships between coffee consumers and coffee creators. Fair trade puts a human face on a cup of coffee, so that instead of an abstract, disinterested approach to consumerism, our purchase takes on a practical implication and our purchasing power is redefined.

Bono's "Red" campaign has shown the efficacy of such business practices. Is it the only solution? Absolutely not. Is it a solution? Yes. According to the Global Fund's website, the Red campaign has raised $195 million to date. Like it or hate it, that's more money than they had a few years ago. The campaign's critics abound. Too much money has been spent on advertising, they say. They pontificate that if people had just donated that "Red" money to the developing world, the net gain would be so much greater. This is all true. But without the campaign, would these same people – the buyers of "Red" products – have given at all?

It is not just a question of money; public opinion must change, and that is a whole project in itself. It is presumptuous even to try to put a price tag on advocacy. How can we ever begin to quantify the lives potentially touched as a result of this or any other kind of awareness-raising campaign? Lost opportunity is lost opportunity. This campaign may be a beginning; let's refine the approach and streamline it, shave off the wasteful practices and get better aid, more funds and more strategic capacity development into the right hands. Anyone who thinks that world poverty will be solved by purchasing a stylish phone or some overpriced clothes is naïve at best. At worst, this is an oversimplification of a very complex problem and a gross understatement of the systemic severity of extreme poverty.

My parents' generation probably didn't consider the implications of their morning cup of coffee and the impact it may have had on others, but things are shifting. Social and economic change is a long-term investment. The dividends cannot be immediately measured, yet we still need to commit. With over a billion people living on less than one Canadian dollar a day, it is a human and moral imperative that we begin to help others onto what Jeffrey Sachs calls the first rung of the economic ladder.[2] His argument, in short, is that unless basic needs are met it is almost an impossibility to rise out of abject, debilitating poverty:

> [T]here are certain places on the planet that, because of various circumstances – geographical isolation, burden of disease, climate, or soil – these countries just can't quite get started. So it's a matter of helping them get started, whether to grow more food or to fight malaria or to handle recurring droughts. Then, once they're on the first rung of the ladder of development, they'll start climbing just like the rest of the world.[3]

As Aristotle has so rightly said, we need to find the balance between excess and defect.[4] We have yet to learn that obscene wealth often leads to obscene waste. Why can't our vast ability to create wealth also include a care and concern that embraces our neighbour? If we agree that it can, and should, then we are well on the way to some kind of systemic transformation. Without that agreement, we are merely ravenous, self-obsessed consumers. We mindlessly devour a lot of goods, and waste plenty as well. If we can slowly begin to alter the current attitude towards what we eat, buy and consume, we can change the world. I take some amount of guarded comfort in the fact that, on some levels, things are improving.

I have heard it said by many Westerners that they don't know what to do. They question how they can make a dent in such an overwhelming problem as global poverty. They wonder about how their daily decisions can affect someone else on the other side of the world. They adopt an attitude often still driven by their own self-interest, saying, "I can't do anything significant about it, so I won't do anything at all." This is a philosophically untenable and morally reprehensible position. Choices are indeed what make us human, and a decision to do nothing still implies choice. We all have a responsibility to act one way or another. I urge you to cast your net.

We can make and are making a difference. This attitude can carry over into everything we do, every decision we make and every word we speak. Knowing and doing are intimately connected: knowledge divorced from action is meaningless. We might meet the Millennium Development Goals[5] if we can nurture a more conscientious approach to something as simple as the kind of coffee we drink. Global poverty may not be ended in our or anyone else's time, but eradicating extreme poverty is an achievable goal. Combat it today and end it tomorrow.

If we merely rely on the "free" market to resolve this issue, then our fiscal complacency has indeed become our moral compass. Commodity-based pricing does not guarantee a fair living wage. Is supply and demand really the only factor that determines price in this so-called free market? I would suggest that there are other things at play here. Who really has the power and influence in the coffee commodity chain? I'm not convinced that the farmer has the clout to make much of a difference. John Talbot argues, in his book *Grounds for Agreement*, that the current market approach to coffee as a commodity is laden with a colonial legacy that makes it hard to find an equitable solution. He writes, "These tropical commodities became important items for mass consumption in the European core at a time when they were produced primarily under the direct control of colonial administrations."[6] These beans, then, were used to feed the massive industrial machine. Stimulants like coffee played an important role in the "revolution," serving to keep the working class sober, alert and productive. In other words, not much has changed when it comes to the green bean.

Oscar Wilde rightly said that "experience is the name that men give to their mistakes." I would like to add, though, that experience often acts as a pathway towards conviction, for every experience is pregnant with meaning. Experience is a good teacher and a marvellous motivator. The difference between isolated, abstract theory and hands-on, direct practice is much like the difference between a photograph and an actual memory. One is mechanical, detached and somewhat inaccessible; the other is full of life, hope and relationship. One imitates, the other resonates.

Experience is priceless. Seeing, touching and feeling others and their needs cannot be replaced by reading a library of books or watching a video store full of film. On-the-ground, tangible encounters are essential to empathy and understanding. One can talk about the disparate economic gap between the North and the South, but if that can also be supported by a bit of concrete experience, the story becomes compelling on so many levels. It becomes relevant, human and important.

Visit a farmer. Watch the documentary *Black Gold*. Empathize with someone else's story. Walk a mile or two in shoes that belong to a young woman who picks coffee beans for a living, and then tell me that the price a Vietnamese, Brazilian or Ethiopian coffee farmer receives for his product is fair. It's really about relationship, and that is why physical and personal contact with others is such an important step towards significant growth and positive change. Touring a farm, sharing a meal or enjoying a cup of coffee with someone in need translates into an empathetic embrace. Compassion leads to understanding and opens doors that would otherwise remain closed. Put a human face on the issue and things will change. Why are we penalizing those without whom our coffee would, for the most part, be inaccessible? To be fair – as in fair trade – is by definition to refrain from exploiting. Fifty percent of our coffee comes from small family businesses, remember; we see only the faceless, austere corporate conglomerate on this end of the commodity chain, not the struggling husband, wife and relatives toiling under a hot and unforgiving sun.

Recently I was involved in a large rural development proposal submitted to the Canadian International Development Agency. I was an integral part of writing a thirty-page document asking the Canadian government to fund a Mongolian literacy program. The charts, the statistics and the editing of the document became a painful experience. I could feel the stress building and the tension mounting as I grew tired of what I believed were insignificant and unnecessary details. The process is driven by what is called "results-based management," and I spent a great deal of time considering who I was calculating "results" for. Was it to benefit the potential donor or the end-of-line stakeholder? The terminology was overbearing and extreme. With each day my cynicism grew like a sprouting, stale onion.

Bam! Then it hit me. I saw the incarnate groups of faces, families and lives that stood at the end of the process, and suddenly this paper-fraught, pencil-pushing, box-filling experience was laden with extraordinary meaning. Lives and personal futures were at stake. And so it is with each product we purchase, each decision we make, each cup of coffee we drink. The resonant power of practical action cannot be underestimated.

The fair trade argument is based on the power of one person – the power of the individual. Ironically, this is one of the tenets of the free market's much-touted and often arrogant claim that the invisible hand of empowered people everywhere will make an economic difference. For the most part, this is true. I believe it. And in the same way, I also believe that fair trade is about empowerment – that it is a living example of the power of one person, one individual choice and one cup of coffee.

Let's turn a bit of economic theory on its head. It seems to me that Schumpeter's notion of creative destruction[7] has to work in more than one way. Innovate and transform – that's what he intended. If the value of established companies is destroyed and they are replaced with a new and potentially more profitable venture, growth may occur. Fair trade has the ability to creatively destroy other less equitable approaches. Call it an innovative approach to creative destruction, or maybe even social transformation based on an economic principle.

The only trouble with such an approach is that it is grounded in ethics, not numbers and economics. The odds of it succeeding are slim at best. Reduce human beings to numbers and it's quite remarkable what equations and answers one will be able to contrive. But there is no moral imperative or incarnate soul attached to numbers. Does the notion of an ethical stance end with us, or does it point to something beyond ourselves and, more importantly, to someone else? The beauty of economic theory based entirely on numerical formulas is that it allows economists the option of ignoring immediate problems. It's all for the greater good, you know. After all, you have to break a few eggs to make an omelet. Indeed! This is, in short, a choice between what is right and what is easy.

Think about the notion of a living transaction. This is coffee with a conscience. It is a metaphor and symbol of a much greater problem, and the potential for a more comprehensive solution. And the market is now broad enough to cover almost everyone's taste buds. Fair trade coffee tastes good! If you're looking for an excuse not to do anything, then you should have stopped reading a few pages ago. You can surely find a reason why you shouldn't do the right thing. But everything we do does indeed affect someone else.

Passion and presence go hand in hand and lead to advocacy of the most important kind. This is not about statistics, numbers and facts, but about justice. Perhaps the kind of free market decision I am advocating could lead to a shift in our collective narrative: our story can become an other story. Maybe, just maybe, it will help us bridge the gap between head and heart.

The breaking of exploitative economic habits cannot be driven merely by fiscal reasoning. If that were the case, nineteenth-century slavery would never have been put on trial. In William Wilberforce's day there were many things created by and through slave labor – the market depended on it to a significant degree. But consumers of the 1800s put their collective fiscal foot down. Sugar cane was one of the first things to suffer from a wide sociopolitical embargo. Big business and opinionated folk argued that this irresponsible financial approach would destroy the economy. Voices could be heard from all levels of society, suggesting that the free market had to be prodded by an invisible hand and not some kind of overarching sense of social justice. The economy would collapse, many feared.

Meanwhile, advertisements in support of the movement to end slavery resembled some of the fair trade labeling we see today: signs indicating that products were produced by "Free Men" could be seen in markets, villages and town squares. Over four hundred thousand people living in London stopped buying sugar that had been picked and produced through slave labour. Those who conducted this boycott had decided to do something about the situation because it was right, not because it would benefit them in the long run. Moral outrage took precedence over an imagined fiscal necessity, and the free market idol was smashed into significant individual and meaningful human pieces.

Adam Hochschild, in his book *Bury the Chains*, on the fight over Britain's enslavement of Africa, writes,

> [Q]uickly, but subversively, the boycott added a new dimension to British political life. At a time when only a small fraction of the population could vote, citizens took upon themselves the power to act when Parliament had not.[8]

To assume that the free market is the only solution to the global issues of our day is a monumental fiction. False gods are prevalent everywhere; it's time we uncovered other aspects of the truth. The market is described as "free," but I'm wondering where we might be able to uncover the inherent oppression and suppression in it. Free in comparison to what and whom?

Many development advocates and authorities have suggested that what is lacking for significant change around the world is collective political will. Bono, Jeffrey Sachs, Stephen Lewis and Paul Hawken have all argued that we have the capability and the technology to end extreme forms of poverty. The coffee we drink can be a metaphorical and practical way of bringing about some global change. It can be a beginning for some of us, like the first necessary step on a ladder. Have you ever tried to use a ladder that is missing the first rung? It's a lawsuit waiting to happen! Skipping the first rung is dangerous, foolish and irresponsible. But assisting others onto that first all-important rung can become a part of who we are and how we live.

My hope is that your passion for basic equality will begin here. Something as simple and necessary as clean water and its provision for others should never be driven by free market ideals; it should be a given! And so should fair trade. To assume trade is fair in and of itself is at best tenuous and at worst perilous. Fair according to whom? Without passion for change, we are climbing a wall with a compromised ladder.

The "tipping point" with respect to global issues presupposes choice, effort and a care and concern for others. Start today; tip tomorrow. The power of our collective human story can be driven by the lives of those who are affected by every cup we drink and every bean we grind.

THIRTEEN

BEAUTIFUL THINGS

"What is important is that each of us begins to trust in our own beauty and our capacity to do beautiful things...when we begin to believe that there is greater joy in working with and for others, rather than just for ourselves, then our society will truly become a place of celebration." —Jean Vanier

I've been travelling to the "majority world" for some time, working on development related projects of one kind or another. I've had the privilege of travelling to Kenya, Cambodia, Indonesia Vietnam and many other countries around our globe. Without a doubt there is no shortage of opportunities for me to love my neighbour here and abroad. The question is: how exactly do I do that?

He called me King David. I returned the royal favour and referred to him as King Josh. I met him many years ago in the town of Eldoret, Kenya, where for four weeks I helped build a medical clinic. I was the electrician; King Josh, the plasterer. He was a delightful guy. Josh was warm and friendly and we did our best to communicate without the benefit of sharing a common language. But I didn't need words to notice that his toes stuck out the end of his shoes. The leather was old and torn, and this made his toes vulnerable to the elements and the harsh realities of a construction site. But he didn't seem to care, and I never heard him complain. I decided to give him the new pair of shoes I had purchased for my trip to Africa. King Josh was thrilled.

However, the next day he arrived back on the job site wearing his old, worn out shoes. I must admit I was a little angry. Had he sold them? Had he given them away? Didn't my gift mean anything to him? My relational immaturity was masked only by my young arrogance. I finally asked him where they were. His response was humbling and enlightening. In the middle of a smile that threatened to envelope his face, he said, "I'm keeping them for good occasions."

So what does it mean to love your neighbour as yourself? It's the second greatest commandment, the Golden Rule, that the church is called to think through, consider and act upon. It fulfills the law. It embodies grace. It is love in action. But it remains challenging for us, as one of the most blessed and opportunity-rich cultures in the world, to follow. After all, what is our prosperity, access and privilege for?

"Everything you do affects someone else." That was what the little note stuck to my mother's refrigerator said. As a youngster I grew up with these little bits of wisdom attached to the door of our fridge. Bible verses and wise quotes from leaders of the past acted as reminders of how to stay on the straight and narrow. Clearly my mother was trying to get through to me. If the usual stuff wasn't working, then perhaps a few strategically placed aphorisms might do the trick.

In the end, my mother's techniques of persuasion worked. I have grown to believe that everything we do affects someone else. We have all heard miraculous, graceful stories of simple, kind acts making all the difference in the world. If it is true that we can have an impact on whomever we engage with and meet, then the individual choices we make each and every moment and each and every day are pregnant with incarnate significance and meaning. C.S. Lewis reminds us that there is no such thing as a *mere mortal*. Everyone counts. Everyone is beautiful. Everyone matters. Sometimes we just have some trouble seeing that beauty.

The twentieth century has shown us through its often violent history that we don't always behave as if we believe in the sanctity of human life as a first principle. We need only think of the tragedy and our lack of response to the men, women and children murdered in the fields of Rwanda, Cambodia or Darfur to see that we sometimes act as if some humans matter more, or less, than others. Living next door has little to do with being a neighbour. We become neighbours by choosing to willingly give love through our actions to others. Proximity is not a factor. Christ confronts us in every person we meet. He does indeed live among us. He is our neighbour, in the poor and displaced, the beggar and the newborn, the needy and the destitute.

Drop a small stone into a still pool of water. There is an initial splash and then the ripples move outwards. One wave affects the other and so on. Cause and effect. The results are significant and can often be awe-inspiring when thinking about the impact our simple actions can have on social and human change. Little things do make a big difference. What, then, are the implications of words, smiles, frowns, tone of voice, handshakes, mentoring, intimate rela-tionships, child sponsorship or spending time with others? They are meaningful actions that on the surface may appear small in quantity, but are significant in quality.

FOURTEEN

ARISTOTLE, MENTORSHIP AND ALEXANDER THE GREAT

"As their mentors, we teach them to take the initiative, to have the moral courage and force that make the difference between followers and leaders. We must, however, demonstrate for them the main points possessed by the leader who travels the determining mile between sporadic and spurious accomplishment and resolute performance in all things." —Wess Roberts

We are all apprentices of one kind or another and can point to significant individuals in our lives that have played the role of mentor, teacher and guide. Professors, relatives, primary school teachers, co-workers, pastors and friends are all examples.

An apprentice is someone who has committed to learning a trade, craft, art or profession over an extended period of time. Apprenticeships always occur within a personal relationship with one or more masters. These masters act as teachers and mentors as knowledge is passed on from one to the other. They guide as they lead. They teach as they mentor. They model as they act.

This Christmas, I was given a book called *The Golden Mean*. It's a piece of historical fiction that tells of the relationship between Aristotle and Alexander the Great. Aristotle was a philosopher with grand metaphysical ideas who probably couldn't have imagined the role he would play in the young Alexander's life. If we recall, Alexander went on to rule much of the modern and known world at the time. His influence was far reaching and the impact of Aristotle's mentoring in his life will never be fully realized, to be sure. When we think of Alexander the Great we do not normally think of him as an apprentice. We think of a ruler, a leader and a man of great power and authority. Perhaps even a mentor in his own right. Yet, he too was guided. Alexander was a nuanced and complex soul. His fiery temperament was complemented by a calmer side. He was perceptive, logical and calculating. He had a great desire for knowledge and a deep love of philosophy. Alexander was an avid reader and was fascinated by wonder. This was, no doubt, in part due to his tutelage by Aristotle.

The Danish philosopher Soren Kierkegaard wrote a short parable called "The Storm," which is a thoughtful reminder of what the wise leader does. It is a story at onceof influence, rigor and responsibility.

> Let us imagine a pilot, and assume that he had passed every examination with distinction, but that he had not as yet been at sea. Imagine him in a storm; he knows everything he ought to do, but he has not known before how terror grips the sea-farer when the stars are lost in the blackness of night; he has not known the sense of impotence that comes when the pilot sees the wheel in his hand become a plaything for the waves; he has not known how the blood rushes to the head when one tries to make calculations at such a moment; in short, he has had no conception of the change that takes place in the knower when he has to apply his knowledge.[1]

This example reminds us that the mentor and the leader engage with one another on many levels. They will become friends. They must relate. They passionately act. The mentor provides the guidance needed to steer the ship. Clearly, Kierkegaard is commenting on the role that experience must play in all of our lives, but through this short narrative he is telling us also how important the leader/mentor relationship will be. The goal, in short, is to lead as taught, and to provide the framework for others to grow.

Prior to becoming a licensed electrician, I served a formal 8500-hour apprenticeship. The lessons learned, more far-reaching than the rules of the trade alone, are innumerable as they are immeasurable. The experience left a long-lasting impact on me. The five-year on-site training helped me to realize that learning happens in those open moments where we allow our hearts and heads to connect, dialogue and interact freely.

Relationships are often difficult, paradoxical and dynamic worlds that we inhabit. Systems cannot anticipate the behaviours or circumstances through which the leader may or may not influence the action of others, but influence they will. These ideas and teachable moments must be seen as launching points for further discussion. They are not the only ten. Indeed they are far from it.

The ten thoughts I propose for your reflection and response are:

1. Action
2. Intention
3. Commitment
4. Self-discipline
5. Gentleness
6. Guidance
7. Kindness

8. Consideration
9. Honesty
10. Relationship

As leaders we are both mentors and apprentices. We guide as we learn. We must remain open to the relationships around us as we seek to situate our mentees in a world that is grounded, yet filled with opportunities to grow and learn more. We mentor the new, the young and the inexperienced, showing them what to expect and how to navigate in their new world. But, in all humility, I believe as leaders we are called to be apprentices also – always learning, pushing ourselves to grow. Plant some seeds in the lives of others, but don't neglect the watering of your own. Our life, in the professional world, is a long series of teachable moments. Grounded in relationship, guided by experience and gifted with insight, we build. We act. We grow.

If we don't mentor, if we choose not to pass on our ideas, our strengths and our collective wisdom, what then?

Experience and the lessons learned will be lost in time. The Pythagorean, pre-Socratic culture of Greece had a strict code of secrecy that was adhered to. They were a superstitious group that gave us much of what we call mathematics today, and yet as a group they were forbidden from talking to others outside of their sect. Sadly, this means that much of their work has been lost to future generations. We have a responsibility to others, as leaders and guides in our fields, to not repeat this mistake.

The goal, then, is to discern when we are teacher and when we are pupil – finding our mentors and learning from them, being found by our mentees and guiding them. As leaders, we must embrace our responsibility to direct the actions of others as they seek to take our place and carry out the purposes of the organization at all levels, while we follow the teachings of our mentors. We preach accountability and we practise flexibility. This is the multi-way street that is mentorship. This is effective leadership.

FIFTEEN

A CAUSAL DISCONNECT

"Millions saw the apple fall, but Newton was the one who asked why." —Bernard Baruch

The term for results-based management[1] is broken. Causal logic was meant to make contact with reality on the ground and in the field, not in a detached, mechanistic and abstract way. It was meant to be effective in creating sustainable change, to leave a lasting impact and make a difference in the lives of men, women and children around the majority world.[2] It's a tool, not the driving force of social change, and a tool that is ineffective needs to be sharpened, adjusted, recalibrated or simply thrown out. "It's the way we've always done things" can never be an excuse for mediocrity.

One of the building blocks of RBM is the "log frame," a two- to three-page document that gives an overview of the key activities of any development project as well as its immediate, intermediate and long-term outcomes. All the writing, thinking and design lead towards one ultimate impact statement, the notion being that

X amount of work and effort will lead to Y amount of change on the ground. This is the causal chain. Unfortunately, however, it is too often seen as a theoretical puzzle that needs solving and not as a process that needs to incorporate actual being and doing. The foundation is a set of numbers and data that can be massaged and manipulated to say this or that. Carried out this way, RBM can become an approach emptied of meaningful relationship and replaced by the filling in of boxes on a chart to create a system that is more concerned with measurement than with making a substantive difference in the field.

We only measure what can be counted, it seems to me, and that's the problem: social transformation cannot be adequately calculated or monitored within the confines of a one-year, three-year or five-year reporting structure. Indicators are important — essential, even. But at what cost do we demand a methodology that can never accurately and holistically record outcomes grounded in human complexity, contradiction and paradox? We are looking for a precision that doesn't exist. The quantification of suffering must always be qualified, because context is everything. People are difficult to understand, geography hard to traverse, and the unknown is a constant: this is the nature of relief and development work. Tangibility and effective impact are things we strive for; we dream of significance and sustainable change. But this is not always realized.

And yet we continue to reach out and beyond, which is precisely what we should be doing. An idealistic and passionate edge is necessary, but so are methodological humility and a hopeful cynicism in view of the vagaries of our day-to-day experience. The need is, and often remains, beyond our current grasp; we may speak in black and white, but on the ground we soon realize that grey tones affect all we see, say and do. Development is about closing the gap, not creating yet another weak link in an already difficult and delicate chain of causal connections.

Numbers and quantification can hypnotize the mind and dazzle the eye of the most savvy donor, corporation or bilateral project partner. We love our facts, figures and statistics, but we lean on them at great cost. Everything in that neat paradigm needs to be seen as a potential for lost opportunity: what or whom might we be excluding because we want things to "add up" in the long run? Two plus two does not always equal four – at least, in the real world it doesn't. Experience has taught us otherwise. At great risk we have equated numbers with meaning and significance. Impact and long-term change become commodities as we calculate costs and ignore the "triple bottom line."[3]

In a recent article in *The Globe and Mail*, Toronto OSPCA lawyer Christopher Avery alleged that the city's local humane society is reluctant to euthanize sick or dying animals when appropriate, and blamed management for dictating policy without taking the animals' best interests into account.

> "What Mr. Trow did is he instituted a policy where the veterinarians, contrary to the regulations and laws that relate to veterinary medicine, aren't able to make the final decision with respect to their patients' medical care," Avery told CBC News. "Euthanasia can only be approved by management, and management seemed more concerned with their euthanasia statistics, because they use them for fundraising purposes, as opposed to the best medical needs of the animals."[4]

Read this out loud and tell me if it makes any sense. How could this have ever become part of the project design? Were questions raised about this as a possible outcome during the humane society's risk assessment? It's unfortunate, but outcomes like this are often the unforeseen conclusion when numbers and donor dollars take precedence. As key motivators, they can eclipse the best of intentions. That's something we need to be sensitive to and aware of. Data-driven decisions come with a cost, one that is different but more important than dollars and PR.

Where is the knowledge we have lost in our passion for mathematical certainty? What of the high relational price tag? In our development projects, are we making judgments based on the sanctity of human life, or are we being driven by the bottom line? Contrary to what Milton Friedman[5] has taught us, the social responsibility of business has never been solely to increase profits. Where is the value of relationship in results-based management? Where is the humanity in logic? How does the causal chain actually connect with reality on the ground? Where is the Other in the most sound and causally connected "log frame"? Or better yet, where should it be?

If we're going to speak and write about costs, capital and causal logic in the context of relief and development, let's at least say it the way it was meant to play out on the ground. We'll continue to challenge the process and rewrite the principles of RBM. Let's upset its mathematical bias and mechanical leaning towards the middle, and continue to push the envelope with the hope for a paradigm shift. It's time for a change of a particular sort.

The future of relief and development work depends on the willingness of RBM decision-makers, at all levels, to participate in new, fresh and comprehensive ways of understanding the development process, infusing it with a regard for others that is holistic, dynamic and eager for sustainable change. The danger of giving precedence to static and manipulable numbers cannot be underestimated. The interdependence of results and human relationship must be allowed to bubble to the surface and make meaningful contact with reality.

The face of the Other does speak.[6] And it compels us to look for opportunities to include, in all of our efforts, the meaning found in the expressions and lives of the men, women and children we serve. We must participate, embrace and include. Otherwise we've lost sight of the driving force behind what we do and the reason we do it.[7]

SIXTEEN

THE UNQUALIFIED POOR

"We have, in fact, two kinds of morality side by side; one which we preach but do not practice, and the other which we practice but seldom preach." —Bertrand Russell

After one of the heaviest rains in remote Cambodia a couple of years ago, unfortunate inmates at a local prison found their cells flooded past their knees. Humanely, prison officials allowed them out to wander the grounds. All but one group. For whatever reason (high flight risk, hardened and dangerous criminals, perhaps), this group of young male teens were kept in their small, locked cells, unable even to sit or lie down. A local NGO working on humanitarian issues at the prison knew it would be two tortuous, sleepless weeks for these men before the water receded. Still they didn't speak up on their behalf. "You have to choose your battles," one prison worker said at the time.

At a time when funds raised are intended for the poorest and most at-risk in our world, development workers are continuously faced with this mantra: pick your battles and help where you can.

Even if it means that those most desperately in need are sometimes excluded. It's a moral quandary that continues to demoralize young people entering the development sector and bother those veterans who wish they could do more with limited resources, rigid reporting frameworks and donor expectations.

Prisoners in some of the worst conditions of extreme poverty in Southeast Asian and African prisons, where officials have metaphorically thrown away the key, often fall within the scope of what Ron Nikkel refers to as the unqualified poor. The president of Prison Fellowship International in Washington, D.C., offers micro-lending programs as an example. These programs work miracles for those who can use them. But a prisoner would never be considered. "As a result, the marginalized are becoming even more marginalized," Nikkel says. Early microenterprise development existed not primarily to make a profit, but for compassionate reasons, and resting on humanitarian principles. When profitability and fundraising take the majority of an organization's time and energy, he suggests they "marginalize the people who probably most need it." Driven by good intentions, they have compromised their initial guiding principles in order to pursue what Nikkel calls a "more comfortable focus," but one that only seems to grow the gap between the poor and the extreme poor. Dr. Samantha Nutt, founder and president of War Child, writes in her book *Damned Nations*, "Rigorous effectiveness measurements are skewed away from high-need groups and towards those more likely to produce maximum results with the imposed timelines. Compromise seeps in everywhere," she suggests, "so that administrative convenience, political ideology, and a bigger is better dogma often receive more attention in decision-making."[1]

Perhaps country music singer Martina McBride got it right when she crooned about burning her house down to get out of a bad relationship, "I'm not saying it's right or wrong, but maybe it's the only way." John Hacker Wright, a philosophy professor from the University of Guelph, says we should have paid more attention in ethics class. He claims it's not about doing what we think we're able to do, but finding out what common ground we share across all cultures to make decisions about solving worst-case problems. "I think we have to clarify our own intuitions about what we think justice is, arrive at a scaffolding, and then present that scaffolding and work from there," he says. And for Wright, Article 1 of the UNHCR is a good foundation as all of us are born equal in dignity and in human rights. Peter Singer, in "Famine, Affluence, and Morality," reminds us that we wouldn't hesitate to help a young child drowning in a pond as we were walking by. He suggests that most of would dive in and help without question. Singer writes, "If it is in our power to prevent something very bad from happening without thereby sacrificing anything else morally significant, we ought, morally, to do it."[2] But that's easier said than done on a grander scale of world aid, says Tanjina Mirza, VP of International Programs for Plan Canada. "Ideally I would love to do everything for everyone, but we can't," she says. "It's not a question about doing. It's a question about doing best." Karen Craggs, a gender specialist from Gender Equality Incorporated, agrees there is no shortage of desire to help directly. "People go to great lengths to do what they do in development, not just because they are passionate, but because it's the moral thing to do," Craggs says. "I think it's the reason why people work in an underpaid sector which often involves working overnight, weekends, and leaving your family."

The realities of serving others can sometimes come down to simple practicalities. "Capacity and financial and geographical reach all have to come into play when dealing with the poorest of the poor," Mirza says. "Decisions have to be made based on the best use of resources and what our organizational understanding of efficacy is." As a starting point, she suggests the old adage: Do no harm. "At Plan, we believe that if we can't do anything of value then we don't do it," claims Mirza. Doing no harm assumes the ability to make good, holistic and wise decisions. It requires that an organization examine its ideas, approaches, and ways of doing development. If the extreme poor are being hurt by judgement calls that help others, those conclusions have to be considered before moving forward. And those decisions, as tough as they can be, and mired in a swamp of moral questions as they are, could be better understood and defined through collective, community knowledge that is at once contextually based, cross-culturally sensitive and gender-focused and has an eye on long-term impact well beyond the tight restrictions of a three- to five-year development project. It's a reality that's tough to accept. But it's also what we count on our development leaders to consider as they guide the course ahead, knowing their decisions could be the difference between leaving the extreme poor behind for another day, or pushing them one more step down the economic ladder. And it will need to be done before a new generation is tainted by the failures of the present, says Jeff Wright. The operations director for Humanitarian and Emergency Affairs for World Vision in Seattle claims the humanitarian community is hurting itself the most in not addressing the issue with young people, who, in seeing those in the most dire need suffering and beyond reach, are simply dropping out. "I see these really bright, young, energetic people, and they're far smarter than me, but they just lack experience and they're thrown into these impossible situations and they're not capable of doing well," says Wright. "The industry chews them up and spits them out."

Dr. Nutt says the same moral failures and poor long-term decision-making are, ironically, affecting the very rich, and are at the root of our worldwide economic recession. "The entire 2008 crash was driven mostly by the failure of ethics, the failure of values, the failure of shared principles, and a failure to even have the most basic of moral compasses," she says. "Maybe we are not schooling our MBAs and our corporate accountants in the right manner." That education and openness is needed among those who are giving their money to development projects too, say critics. Ian Smillie, a consultant, writer and development specialist, says that one of the big problems in the field is our unwillingness to come clean about our methods and the true nature of systemic change. "We've told them that development is quick and easy. Just give us the money and we'll get the job done. But it isn't quick and it isn't easy, and it's very complicated," says Smillie. "It's very messy and we don't always know what we're doing. A lot of it is risky and experimental, and there's nothing wrong with that as long as we learn from what we're doing." Smillie and others agree on the need to keep talking – the need to keep asking ourselves questions in a sincere attempt to understand the field, to have a more sustainable long-term impact.

Having a healthy, robust and focused discussion around critical issues can and often does lead to change and to action. Our hearts, for the most part, are in the right place. But whether the next shut-in Cambodian prisoner, up to his knees in water with no end in sight, will be able to survive our good intentions will be what haunts us even as we continue to spread our successes elsewhere.

SEVENTEEN

THE FACE, FORGIVENESS
AND THE OTHER

"The belief in a supernatural source of evil is not necessary: men alone are quite capable of every wickedness." —Joseph Conrad

Roméo Dallaire's book *Shake Hands with the Devil* changed my life. I had just finished reading *Race Against Time* by Stephen Lewis and was clearly in a social-justice frame of mind.

General Dallaire was leading the UN Peacekeeping Mission in Kigali at the time of the Rwandan Genocide. He was advocating for international intervention, but the world was not listening. Dallaire's message, in short, was the lesson to be drawn from the inaction and indifference of the West: some human beings are simply more important than others.[1]

While reading his harrowing historical account of the events leading up to the one hundred days of horror in 1994, I came across an advertisement for a position as an instructor in a postgraduate international development program. It read: "The Hardest Job of Them all – Changing the World." I applied and was accepted. I now teach at the school where, as a student, I discovered a world that included other cultures, creativity and communities: thirty-two languages were represented in the class I attended. My eyes opened wider. As well, I am now working in the field of international development myself and have founded SoChange,[2] a capacity-building organization that empowers NGOs (non-governmental organizations) in the majority world.

On a recent trip to Rwanda I spent five days in Kigali and a little bit of time working with an NGO[3] that was doing significant work in reconciliation, restorative justice and forgiveness. Although this experience was life-changing, it was brief and very limited. And so it seems to me that what follows, the writing that I have done on this issue, is in some regard rather academic. The divide between theory and praxis has narrowed for me, in a way, because I've had a chance to observe; but at the same time it has widened, because that brief contact revealed a gaping abyss between the little I know and the enormous reality I have yet to experience.

A POISON TREE

I was angry with my friend,
I told my wrath, my wrath did end,
I was angry with my foe,
I told it not, my wrath did grow.

And I watered it in fears,
Night and morning with my tears,
And I sunned it with smiles,
and with soft deceitful wiles.

And it grew both day and night,
'Til it bore an apple bright,
And my foe beheld its shine,
And he knew that it was mine.

And into my garden stole,
When the night had veiled the pole,
In the morning glad I see,
My foe outstretched beneath the tree.[4]

For instance, I met a man who had murdered seven Rwandans –
Tutsi men and women that he had hacked to death with a machete.
Some of them may have been friends or family. His name is Jean
de Dieu, which means "John of God." He shook hands with me.
Standing face to face, we smiled and talked. He is evidence of
the reparation occurring as a result of a comprehensive national
campaign dealing with nationwide forgiveness. He now works for
a local NGO as a security guard. Irony? Indeed. I met many people
like Jean. I visited a reconciliation village where Rwandans are
working hand in hand to rebuild communities and, presumably,
their lives.

In a village meeting where a victim and an offender told me their
painful stories, I was humbled and astonished at the desire of the
community in Ruhengeri province to work through their responsibility to themselves and to others. An older woman grabbed me by
the right hand and held on tight. We were surrounded by villagers.
It was a visceral, refreshing experience I won't forget. She then gra-
ciously grabbed both my hands, looked into my eyes and held on
tighter. Face to face she smiled at me. I returned the gesture and
was moved to tears that were well hidden behind my overpriced

Ray-Bans. I was reminded of an ancient Chinese proverb: "*The one who pursues revenge should dig two graves.*"

I have six main points to make about ethics, the Other and forgiveness, inspired partly by philosopher Emmanuel Lévinas and others:

1. Our responsibility to the Other begins in the face-to-face encounter. For Lévinas this is a first philosophy.[5]

2. Forgiveness is always practised within a community. As Lévinas reminds us, in facing one, I face everyone.[6]

3. Forgiveness is about living and acting well.

4. To avoid forgiveness is to run from our freedom.[7]

5. Forgiveness is situated in self-interest, but only – as Lévinas reminds us – in an ethical and asymmetrical fashion.[8] In other words, the Other counts more than me. In being for the Other, we are in a sense being for ourselves.

6. The Other is then grounded in a relationship of intersubjectivity and inner dependence. In *The Wisdom of Forgiveness* the Dalai Lama reminds us that "the theory of inner dependence allows us to develop a wider perspective and, with a wider mind, less attachment to destructive emotions like anger and therefore more forgiveness."[9]

Cambodia is a country that has been ravaged by civil war, international ignorance and genocide. The Killing Fields tell a grim story; like Rwandans in the 1990s, Cambodians were killing their countrymen in the mid-1970s. In her book *First They Killed My Father*, in a chapter entitled "The Execution," Loung Ung tells a gripping and horrific story as a thirty-year-old woman recollecting her experience through the lens of a nine-year-old girl.

In her village a local Khmer Rouge cadre leader had been captured. The villagers banded together, appeared at the prison carrying clubs, sharp stakes, knives, axes and hammers, and called for his release so they could wreak revenge on him. Punitive justice was their goal. The jailors buckled under the collective local pressure and released this genocidaire to the cheers of the crowd, who grabbed him and took him to the centre of the village. Once surrounded he was tied to a chair. Ung recalls the emotions she felt as a child. She writes about a sense of satisfaction at what she was about to witness. At nine years old she understood the notion of blood for blood. Eyes for eyes.

The villagers were talking about how they were going to evoke a vengeful, slow and painful death on this Khmer Rouge leader. They were specific in their bloody desire for retribution. Local leaders asked for volunteers to come forward and kill the man. Two women emerged from the crowd, the younger holding a hammer, the older a long, rusty knife. Weapons in hand, one woman spoke about losing her children and husband, the other about her whole family motherless and grandmotherless. The nine-year-old child describes the horrific, bloody sight as these two women slowly kill the man. Covered in blood as they walked away from the mangled corpse, these two women reminded her of death. Only their eyes looked alive, she recalls, but it was with anger, rage and hate. She writes,

> There he is, I stand and I find myself almost face to face with him, separated by only fifteen feet. Automatically I raise my scarf to cover my head and my face. My heart beats wildly, fear seeps into my body. He is looking at me. He can see me.[10]

How does one meaningfully speak and write of forgiveness in a context such as this? Theory and praxis? How does one close the divide?

Lévinas tells us that because of Auschwitz all of Western philosophy and religion has failed. This breakdown occurred precisely because it privileged knowledge over ethics.[11] After over a hundred million dead in the twentieth century, it seems to me that we can reasonably ask, why things are the way they are and not some other way.

Like the writings of any great thinker, Lévinas' work is dominated by one major thought. Richard Bernstein likens his thinking to a wave on a beach, always returning as it softly falls on the shore, repeating its movement with a deeper and more resonant impact.[12] For Lévinas, ethics is first philosophy. It is considered and understood as a relation of infinite responsibility to the other person. There is no argument here. He does not attempt the axiomatic precision of Spinoza's ethics; there is no need. The Other just *is*. "Goodness consists in taking up a position such that the Other counts more than myself,"[13] he writes. His most memorable statement is: "The face speaks." And what it says to us is: "Thou shall not kill."[14] The face has meaning and does not depend on anything else for its meaning.

Lévinas does not begin with epistemology, ontology or cosmology, but with the notion of the Other. Method is transcended in favour of relationship. The essence of his critique of Western philosophy is that it has reduced the Other to an "objective same"; that is, it has objectified the Other and in so doing robbed the Other of uniqueness and individuality. Our neighbour is no longer our neighbour, another human person with a face, but only the featureless exemplar of a class, an ethnic group, a race, a party.

As a phenomenologist Lévinas was trying to seek out, identify and analyze shared features of our average everyday experience. Searching for those relational reminders of what we already know,[15] Lévinas is not looking for empirical data, a utilitarian starting point or ontological structure. He wants to make explicit what he believes is embedded in our ordinary, everyday existence: a tacit understanding, a relational apprehension as opposed to an epistemic comprehension. It is in this way that we indwell the Other. The face speaks, and what it says is "thou shall not kill." We are responsible. We are in relationship to the Other. As John Russon writes in *Human Experience*, "We will see that the issue of other people is not simply one issue among many, but it is rather the issue that sets the terms for all our dealings."[16] To respond responsibly to the face of the Other is to take care of the Other's needs. To recognize the Other is to give. "Each of us is responsible before everyone, for everyone, and I more than the rest."[17]

Simone de Beauvoir understands the Other. As a twentieth-century existentialist, she is responding to Nietzsche's notion that Zarathustra's god is now dead.[18] She emphasizes the primacy of individual existence over any kind of natural essence for human beings. We have the radical freedom to make of ourselves whatever we will. With this humanity, though, comes the incredible and daunting responsibility of employing that freedom appropriately. And it must be done without escaping into the inauthenticity or self-deception of any conventional set of rules for our behaviour; choice, she says, is inescapable. Lévinas would agree. The human being must be free, and although we are bound to some extent by circumstance, all else is up to the individual. De Beauvoir argues in *The Ethics of Ambiguity* that one can face up to one's freedom or try to escape it. It's easy to pretend; it's easy to hide under the banner of determinism, where we are free to ignore the subjectivity of our own choice.[19] Freedom, like the Other, is indeed hard to face.

"Man's unhappiness is first due to his having been a child," says Descartes.[20] At birth we are thrown into a world not of our own making. This brings on the anxiety, the fear and the angst that causes us to run from our freedom. We hide elsewhere and ulti-mately avoid our responsibility to the Other.

De Beauvoir writes against this flight and insists that the freedom of any individual is dependent on the freedom of the Other.[21] Human encounters confirm the connection between one's own freedom and that of the Other. We do not exist for ourselves only. We are defined through our relationships to other people. Being, for de Beauvoir, is social and relational, and therefore it is impossible for the individual to regard only herself in her ethical choices. That is to say, since people live together in community, even though they may create their own values, they cannot disregard the existence of those around them. We are free, but we are free for others and as a result we have a moral obligation to them. "To will oneself free is to will others free. This will is not an abstract formula. It points out to each person concrete action to be achieved."[22] Human agency, action and the Other are connected in a primary way.

De Beauvoir asks us to respond to the freedom of the face-to-face encounter. She pleads with us to choose and act responsibly. I believe that the face of the Other implores us to acknowledge, accept and actively pursue the freedom found in forgiveness. Levinas argues that we cannot choose to be responsible, but we can choose to act responsibly.[23] The will has no option but to be respon-sible. Forgiveness asks and relationally encourages us to choose and recognize others. If we objectify the face, we ignore the moral imperative inherent in the fact of otherness. De Beauvoir's notions of radical freedom and responsibility come into clarity here: the face-to-face encounter is crystallized in her understanding of the Other. There is no prescription; we choose forgiveness simply because the face speaks. Accepting the Other necessarily opens us up to saying "I pardon you." To forgive is to *choose* to do so.

It seems to me that absolution and authenticity are connected: genuine forgiveness is essential to being fully human; it's about living and acting well. To choose not to forgive is to run from what makes us free, responsible and relational beings.

The night before I left Rwanda, Dio Jean, another Rwandan, told me his story in the lobby of the Chez Lando hotel in Kigali. He was fourteen years old when, during the Genocide, members of the Rwandan Patriotic Front found him hiding by the river. His feet were "like elephants," he recalled, describing the severity of swelling due to malnutrition. In a compelling and passionate way, he told me how the soldiers said he could either go to a refugee camp on the border of the Democratic Republic of the Congo or come with them. At fourteen he picked up an AK-47, fought the Hutu extremists and helped to bring some kind of order back to Rwanda. I asked him about Ubuntu. Ubuntu is an ethical notion originating in African culture.[24] In essence, it reminds us that a person is a person because of other people: my humanity is caught up with your humanity. "I was angry with my friend. I told my wrath, my wrath did end."

We live moving forward, wrote Kierkegaard. We understand looking backward.

And it was Niebuhr who famously wrote:

> Nothing worth doing is completed in our lifetime, therefore we are saved by hope; nothing true or beautiful or good makes complete sense in any immediate context of history, therefore we are saved by faith; nothing we do, however virtuous, can be accomplished alone, therefore we are saved by love; no virtuous act is quite a virtuous act from the standpoint of our friend or

foe as from our own; therefore we are saved by the final form of love which is forgiveness.[25]

Oscar Wilde is without a doubt one of my favourite writers. He understood social injustice. In his magnificent poem "The Ballad of Reading Jail" he wrote of judgment, hypocrisy and forgiveness.[26] He knew a little about anger and a great deal about biting satire. In a wonderful turn of phrase, Wilde delivers this reminder: "Always forgive your enemies; nothing annoys them so much."[27]

EIGHTEEN

SEPSIS AND SAGE ADVICE

"Since I am coming to that holy room, / Where with thy choir of saints for evermore / I shall be made thy music." —John Donne

George Bernard Shaw said, "Life is no brief candle to me. It is a sort of splendid torch which I am permitted to hold for the moment, and I want to make it burn as brightly as possible before handing it on to future generations." Kind of sounds like Roy Batty's iconic and mythological speech at the end of Bladerunner. "I've seen things you people wouldn't believe..."

My father has Parkinson's disease. He's been diagnosed now for almost thirty years. I remember the night my parents told my brother and me. We didn't take it too well. They had been hiding the news from us for several years. Mom and Dad had their reasons that probably seemed good to them at the time, but we weren't buying it. My mother, Nancy, made us a lemon meringue pie, thinking maybe that it would help to lighten the emotional family blow. It didn't. I feel foolish today because of my behaviour back then, but I didn't stick around. I was angry. I was confused about

Parkinson's. Was it fatal? Was it hereditary? I felt so betrayed and alienated from my parents. I saw it as an issue of trust. I drove to a friend's house and we chatted for hours, sitting on undersized kiddie swings in his Streetsville backyard. I don't find myself crying very often, but I did that night. It's the only time my brother and I have shared something so closely. It was in the front seat of my red Pontiac Sunbird. After hearing the news, I burst out the front door of our house in anger. He followed me out to the street and there we sat talking about the implications in tears together. What a shitty car.

It's been a long, hard road. That's an understatement. They say caregivers take an emotional and physical beating, and in my mother's case it's true. She's tired. She's worn out and emotionally and spiritually drained. They both deserve medals. We give out golds to athletes who win a race by a millisecond. How about awards for those folks in society who have gone the extra mile in almost every way? Married for fifty-two years, they both signed on for more than they bargained for. In sickness and health? My parents have had more of one than the other.

Neurological diseases are slow and painful to watch and, I would imagine, to endure. Unlike other illnesses that squeeze the life out of their patients fairly quickly, chronic diseases take their time as the senses are worn down and slowly the mind and body fail. Like whittling a hundred-year-old oak tree down with a dull Swiss army knife. Slow, painful and seemingly meaningless. I've heard my father say, "It's time to leave this life," and ask deep existential questions like, "What have I done of value?" Under the influence of morphine, he told me once that he didn't feel his life had added up to much. I don't remember what I said, but I tried to affirm in some way, I'm sure. Looking back, I don't think he would really agree with that notion anymore, but I had to wonder where it came from. Were these comments coming from a drug-addled mind or someone facing a harsh reality that was just bubbling to the surface? A truth about his life or a half truth filtered through the physiological shock of psychedelic drugs? If my dad were a drinker I bet he would have been a chatty, philosophical drunk. He's a gentle, silent kind of guy for the most part. Opinionated, but private. A sharp thinker, but reserved. He has a subtle, dry humour that is occasionally revealed at family events. Overnight my dad went from Cavett to Camus. Amazing what a little dope can do. It's the quiet guys, I guess.

This was also around the same time he told me that the little things were getting difficult to manage. Apparently blowing his nose was now a big problem. I brought him some Rolo chocolates one afternoon. My dad loves anything sweet and yet he could barely open the package. Unheard of for Mr. Peck. His energy was sapped and his behaviour so unlike the father I knew. That same day I asked him to sign his name on my mother's birthday card. The celebration was around the corner. Holding the pen was a challenge, scribbling down a cursive, unreadable *H* almost impossible. He managed to fight his way through it, but it was excruciating to watch. So this is what happens to us as we age and fall apart at the seams. Dad was struggling, to say the least. Climbing dysfunctional neuro-mountains that others have yet to face and that many will never have to.

In some regards my mom was having a more difficult time than my dad as she looked for answers, prayed incessantly for a recovery of some kind and continued to attend and care for his simple, bodily needs. The ordeal of living with my father's disease has stretched her in unimaginable ways. She has walked emotional and spiritual roads that are often desolate and lonely, sometimes filled with pain, guilt and regret. It's hard to know how to help, how best to come alongside and support someone so close. Ironic, but in some ways it might be easier to uplift a stranger. How odd we humans are. My mom needs a rest. Having never taken a holiday from my dad physically or emotionally, she is tapped out. Who wouldn't be? In her own way, she has redefined perseverance. I just wish sometimes that Mom could see the sun a little more often, but who am I to judge a woman who has gone the extra mile more often than not. She continues to plod ahead, rolling the rock up the proverbial hill, eagerly awaiting better and brighter days. Hope can be a dangerous thing. My mom just doesn't smile very much anymore. I wonder if the muscles that operate in the face that allow us to smile atrophy the more disillusioned, disheartened and detached we become?

These last few years have allowed me to see things from a new perspective – sometimes experiencing fresh, vibrant light shining in the darkness. Grace comes to us in mysterious ways. My dad doesn't read newspapers anymore. Not because his mind can't handle the words, concepts or ideas, but because he can't physically make it work. He lacks the motor skills. The neurons in his brain are disabled by a deficiency of dopamine required for the stuff of "normal" daily neurological operations. It's like watching a marathon runner prepare for a long race with his feet tied together. My dad's patience, tenacity and stiff British upper lip shine through in moments like these. The paper moves around like loose, windblown leaves as he struggles, trying desperately to right and balance the impossible to handle pages of the newspaper. A simple task now unattainable. A former, everyday occurrence turned into a chore like a circus act. It would be hard to re-enact, but Laurel and Hardy could recreate the moment for sure. Maybe Deniro as well. He was good in *Awakenings*. It's almost comical to watch and would make for a good YouTube video if it wasn't so tragic and if it wasn't my dad. I've watched him closely many times as he eats his meals. At family events we can all be finished with a long, tasty dinner and be in the process of cleaning up, and my dad is still struggling through the first course. The table has been cleared of plates, cutlery and condiments and my dad is still hunched over the dish. Forty-five minutes to finish a bowl of soup. I timed it one evening. Watching him butter a roll can be torturous. The knife, crumbs and bun land in various spots and positions on the table, his lap and floor as Dad is determined to make it work. I'm caught between wanting to help, needing to step in, and giving him the respect and freedom he deserves to try to still do it himself.

He told me a few years ago after a long hospital stay while recovering from a cervical laminectomy that he'd been to hell and back. Some of the discs in his spine were bulging and buckling and pinching nerves in his spinal cord, causing him serious pain. Dr. Lee, a brilliant neuro-surgeon, cut a twelve-inch incision in his back and screwed two titanium rods into his body to help him deal with what's called cervical spinal stenosis. I think on some level they were treating my dad like a bit of a guinea pig. I joked with the doctor about how he might be able to publish the results in a medical journal if things went as planned. He smiled a little, and my dad didn't seem to mind being the specimen in a fresh new, scientific experiment. The rods run down his spine from the base of his brain stem. As a result, he can no longer turn his neck left or right. It's like he's wearing a permanent brace. He now has to move his body at the hips to turn his head. Another sign of the long and dreary process of decay. The surgery was dangerous. The recovery was long and scary. I left for Indonesia on business a few days later and landed to an e-mail from my brother. "Dad's got an infection." My father has always said, "Worse things happen at sea." It's probably true, but I know my mother feels we've been on the waves for way too long now. In fact, she tells me that he doesn't say that much anymore.

Many times I visited him in the hospital it looked like he wasn't going to recover. The cognitive dissonance, raging incoherence and gaunt colour of his skin were good indicators of even more challenging days to come. The incision took ages to heal. He was often quite emotional and would shed a few tears over what seemed to be fairly insignificant issues at the time. He was clearly experiencing a drug-induced epiphany of sorts. Like an Old Testament prophet he told me many times that "God is good. God is great. God is love." Sounds like something a fundamentalist terrorist might say while building an explosive roadside device. I would sometimes leave the hospital feeling unsettled, upset and undone, yet still smiling at the paradox and contradictions of life. I often wished that I still smoked too.

The antibiotics wreaked havoc on my dad's body and the narcotics took his mind to new places. Pills worked for Huxley's creativity. They also had an impact on my dad's. I called it coherent madness at the time. Cognition and perception were fully and clearly altered. I remember him swearing that he saw hundreds of busy, big, black bugs on the ceiling. The look on his face made me realize he was serious. I didn't see any insects at all. Nothing. Of course he claimed they were everywhere. Dad pointed, got angry with me and said I was lazy and that I wasn't looking closely enough. A cocktail of morphine, Percocet and Tylenol 3's along with his twenty-seven different Parkinson's medications were taking their toll. What is this *Naked Lunch*? William Burroughs, Franz Kafka and

Hunter S. Thompson made more sense. My dad's funnier, though. He spent three months in hospital this time around as he recovered from the operation and the infection. Ninety-two days and nights. He's been through the wringer, back home and through the wringer again. Several times. My dad personifies the meaning of trooper. He rarely complains and willingly perseveres. Not sure why, but there is something honourable and slightly infuriating about his patient resolve to take it all with a small dose of temperance and in a day-by-day way that I sometimes simply don't understand.

I visited often and heard stories. Wonderful stories. He had long, detailed accounts about things that went bump in the night. How he shouted directions and assertive commentary to his roommate next to him and occasionally yelled at other patients across the hall. The nurses seemed to like my father and since the infection he was getting extra special attention, but no doubt they hand their hands full. On the surface it looked like he was losing his mind, but some of his moments had such clarity to them it was remarkable. Lucidity comes with a cost. Many nights on driving away from the hospital I wondered which dad was mine. Pre or post narcotic. I found out later that a few of the nighttime tales weren't fiction after all. There was some truth there. He could often be heard through the halls at night, shouting scripture and aphoristic words of wisdom, quoted, no doubt, with care and testimonial accuracy.

On one of my earlier visits he had invented a new game based on the alphabet. The idea was to pick a letter and choose a word beginning with that same letter. Then look for its opposite. He had no name for it, but seemed to enjoy the mental gymnastics of it all. Coherent madness. Like a wasp on a summer picnic, out of nowhere and sometimes with a sting. These moments could come and go all in one visit and in a matter of minutes. Kind of Jekyll and

Hyde like. "Start with the letter D," my dad said. "The Devil. Now find its opposite – God. Or C for Churchill and find its opposite. Hitler." It took me quite a while to figure out the rules of the game as I really had no idea what my father was talking about. It sounded like absolute gibberish. Then I understood how the game was played. He was acting like a serious Dr. Seuss. Making sense in his own mind and eventually to me as well, once I realized he wasn't messing around. "It's just the use of words," he said. "I can do it and I'm pretty stupid."

I come from a very conservative background and am truly grateful for much of what I learned as a child. Great lessons and good memories while growing up. Solid foundations were laid for the most part, but I'm not so crazy about some of the finer details of my younger years and the accompanying formative footnotes. Like, for instance, how I was taught by parents, church and school that my mind and body were disconnected. Dualism rears its ugly head once again. Don't trust your body, I was told. Yoda called it crude matter. Even Star Wars can't escape the grip of Plato. The message was loud and clear that my body was a merely a disposable husk for my soul. Heart knowledge was interesting and to be applauded in some way, but head knowledge mattered more. I've paid a price for the split. This is not just the stuff of academic, theoretical philosophy, but where one's worldview makes contact with reality in meaningful ways. I often struggle to exist in the present. It's hard to be here in the now. Sometimes while pondering even the thought of the moment, I've already moved onto what's next. I've lived a disconnected life in many regards. I think my father has too. And so, while I was sitting on his hospital bed, we stepped into new territory, together exploring the cosmos and looking closely at the universe's whys, whats and hows and our place in it. Dad was asking questions, out loud, that I hadn't imagined he had even considered, never mind would admit to his forty-four-year-old philosophy major son. We talked about prayer and the omnipotence of God. He wanted to know why some people's requests were granted while others were met with silence. He questioned whether or not God really was all-powerful. We talked about the deity as a cosmic slot machine. He was interested in the classic problem of evil and, being a child of the Second World War, wanted to know whether the God the German pilots' mothers prayed to was the same as the God "a good old Luton boy's" mom prayed to. Same God, no doubt. After seventy years Dad was finally starting to come clean. "So they wind up in a dog fight over Germany," says my father. "Who dies?" "Dad," I said one evening after about ninety minutes of some fairly interesting and tough questions, "That's why I chose to study philosophy. I wanted to try and work some of this stuff out." He looked at me without missing a beat and said, "Well, it seems to have worked out pretty well for you." It's the only time I remember my father so blatantly and willingly affirm me. Ever.

I also had the kind of upbringing that looked down on drinking, smoking, dancing and loud rock music – essentially everything that many young people believe to be fun. Tools of the devil, you know. So hearing and watching my dad speak and behave in this way was unsettling at best. He was an elder of a conservative church assembly of Bible believers, not a doped up "crazy," with spurts of creative genius and a hundred surgical staples in his back. An angry tone one moment and shouting at someone the next. Some of it was tough to listen to. Always so odd and hard to reconcile every time I would visit. He told me wild, absurd things about nurses hitting on him at night, "carrying on" and standing on his bed. Some of it was crazy, violent stuff. Plenty of disturbing images and ideas that I've decided to keep to myself. It's between me and my dad.

Shaw was right. Life is a splendid torch. I just wish it wouldn't have to burn out so quickly or, as in some cases, maybe not quickly enough. The cradle to the grave realities I still sometimes just don't get. It's a crummy design, if you ask me. Getting old may indeed be part of the circle of life, but I don't have to like it.

My father told me wonderful things. That he "wanted to take the conversation higher," and that in life we need to be reminded of "how tough this game can get." He came up with marvellous ideas about sermons he was going to preach and how we all need to be grateful for the little things. "We've got to share our problems and good things in life together," Dad told me. Sage advice from a guy who, if found on the street, might have been jailed for being under the influence.

During his hospital stay he seemed to be going though an awakening of sorts – a spiritual journey – a recovery during his recovery. I know that his words and thoughts were filtered through his swamp-water-like mix of narcotics, painkillers and yummy hospital food, but you know what? He's still my dad. Wisdom I never thought I would hear coming from the heart and soul of my father. Memories, questions and words I will always have with me until my own system starts to deteriorate, depreciate and decline.

Recuperating from acute sepsis and in a post-surgical hallu-cinogenic freedom, my dad broke down a barrier or two and we made some major connections. I told him I loved him almost every visit. I'm not the demonstrative type, especially with my parents. It seems we're just not that kind of family and yet Brecht's fourth wall vanished during those three long months as we built new bridges and gained some serious relational ground. We may have even begun to dismantle a fifth one together. Time, recollections and conversation together will tell.

A few of the greatest and most important chats I've ever had with my father were during his long-term hospital stay. His experience and understanding of it have given me a new appreciation for the frailty of life, each beautiful moment we have and of course for my parents. They do warrant medals. More than medals. They deserve our love, respect, attention and care for who they are, what they've taught us, getting through it all together and for just plain getting it all done.

NINETEEN

MADE LOVE. WAR'S BETTER.

"There are many causes I would die for. There is not a single cause I would kill for." —Mahatma Gandhi

Here are 800,000 reasons why I'm not a pacifist. Pacifism is a sometimes troubling, lofty thought experiment. It's an ideal to work towards. It's worth hoping for. It's often out beyond our grasp. Once in a while discussion, dialogue and the relational approach have to wait in favour of more radical solutions. Pacifism for most of us is an over privileged, theoretical tug of war. We get to play philosopher and part time, pseudo, wannnabe Mennonite while we rarely if ever have to deal with the real, foundational issues that ultimately make pacifism sometimes morally reprehensible.

I get it. I understand the notion and the theory. It just doesn't always work. It lacks a nuance or two that considers my family, my children, human trafficking, child soldiers and other global and personal concerns. Where does it all begin and end?

I'm all for it, but getting the theory off of your Bible, Koran or Torah like paper and onto the bloody ground around the world changes things, it seems to me. Wish it were simpler.

Guns, punching back and anger are not the answer. Violence is not the answer. Dialogue and restorative justice are the way forward. I'm on board and I believe in pacifistic principles. The BBC tells me I live in a world that doesn't always agree. I like the idea of pacifism. I will spread the word and speak hopefully about standing down, but will consider other options if and when the time comes that it's a fundamental necessity. The problem is who decides. When article one of the UNDHR has been ignored and others are at risk of losing their choice, their autonomy and maybe their lives, I believe I am morally obligated to act. If I'm not then who is? If someone punches me for no reason at a rowdy book release party where the wine and weirdness are flowing, I can say almost without a doubt I will act neighborly, pacifistically and relationally. The Golden Rule helps here. I will be as friendly as someone can be with a fat lip and a bloody nose. However, threaten my wife, Elizabeth, my children, or someone else or their children, and my ethics and principles stay the same but the practical reality I then face makes all the difference. The disconnect between theory and practice is, in the moment, more than relevant. Are kidnappers, rapists, the LRA or those willing to exploit children around the world open to a friendly, Starbucks-like chit chat? Is standing idly by and turning the other cheek not also a moral act? When do we say enough? To restore any relationship requires a commitment on all sides.

I'm all for beating swords into ploughshares, but not sure they have much to do with changing the ideological leanings of the US in Vietnam, the Khmer Rouge in Cambodia or those responsible for the 800,000 dead in Rwanda. These real world examples make contact with reality in ways we here in the West for the most part will read, reflect on or philosophize about.

I am a pacifist. Just of the hope so kind.

TWENTY

FOR THE TIME BEING

"The country is in deep trouble. We've forgotten that a rich life consists fundamentally of serving others, trying to leave the world a little better than you found it. We need the courage to question the powers that be, the courage to be impatient with evil and patient with people, the courage to fight for social justice. In many instances we will be stepping out on nothing, and just hoping to land on something. But that's the struggle. To live is to wrestle with despair, yet never allow despair to have the last word." —Cornel West

I believe in social justice and transformation. I believe in radical, relational revolution of all kinds. Today and tomorrow are meaningless if we're not grounded in a past that we can remember and if we can't make some sense of a future that will matter. Let's move forward, fail, fall down, get up and move on. We can do it together, regardless of religion, worldview or sexual orientation.

We need to apprehend and not just comprehend. Movement presupposes change, choice and responsibility. Freedom links us to the past but allows us to reach out into the future and stand with a proper confidence on the edge of any kind of unsettling uncertainty and what's next.

We need definitions that resonate and make contact with reality in multiple and meaningful ways. We need relationships.

This is not about a radical, class-based, Marxist critique of power structures and ideological inklings. This is about real people. Social justice begins by realizing that we all drink the same water from the same well. And as Peter Singer has written in *Famine, Affluence and Morality*, "if it is in our power to prevent something bad from happening, without thereby sacrificing anything of comparable moral importance, we ought, morally, to do it."

Social justice is inclusive. It's hopeful. It's uplifting and is grounded in a care and concern rooted in and for the Other. Love your neighbour as yourself is the foundation for the Universal Declaration of Human Rights. Assume nothing other than the Other matters more. The strength behind a desire for social, sustainable change is found in its holistic understanding that every human being matters. And that lack of opportunity is the antithesis of all that is good, beautiful and true.

Social justice avoids the easy, cynical and passive response and proclaims that we will make a difference. Let us live passionately, act intentionally and commit to the redemptive side of our humanity that says to others, "You're included." Life then is not a goal to be achieved, but a way to live, move and have our being.

TWENTY-ONE

PRACTICAL ACTION

"Knowledge is of no value unless you put it into practice."
—Anton Chekov

This is the longest essay in the book: over fifty pages. So giddy up. I think Charles Dickens may have had introductions that were longer, but alas, we are in a different age. The essay started as my Master's thesis in philosophy and so may seem a bit too academic; I've tried to make it as readable and accessible as possible, but would imagine I have failed for some. Skip it if you find it a little overwrought as you dig in, but I believe you will find lessons here that are invaluable and applicable to the average and the everyday. The thesis was the culmination of a study of knowledge and its relationship to what we do and how we do it. I was reminded once again during my academic studies that the power of real change is to be found in the baby steps and the little things. Knowing is about doing. Knowing ourselves is about practical, intentional action, and therefore we must always come back to freedom, choice and responsibility.

> **knowl·edge – noun**
>
> Epistemology (from the Greek επιστήμη – epistēmē, meaning "knowledge, understanding," and λόγος – *logos*, meaning "study of") is the branch of philosophy concerned with the nature and scope of knowledge and is also referred to as "theory of knowledge." It questions what knowledge is and how it can be acquired, and the extent to which any given subject or entity can be known.

1. Information and skills acquired through experience or education

2. The theoretical or practical understanding of a subject.

3. What is known in a particular field or in total – the facts and information.

4. Acquaintance with facts, truths or principles, as from study or investigation.

5. General erudition. The knowledge of many things.

6. Familiarity or conversance, as with a particular subject or branch of learning.

7. Acquaintance or familiarity gained by sight, experience, or report.

8. Knowledge of human nature.

9. The fact or state of knowing.

10. The perception of fact or truth.

11. Clear and certain mental apprehension.

12. Awareness, as of a fact or circumstance.

13. The fact or condition of knowing something with familiarity gained through experience or association.

This essay is about what we know, what we do and what we think we can do. An adequate understanding of the world around us precedes our ability to act in a deliberate and passionate way. My hope is that your regard for the little things that make up what we know will affect how you see the world and how you behave in it – towards the earth, and more importantly towards your neighbour, both at home and abroad. The building blocks that add up to our everyday and sometimes seemingly insignificant experience can and do make all the difference.

I am a perpetual student. I've been captured by wonder in every sense of the word, by experience and by emotion. Life, for me, is like a two-for-one sale at a used bookstore (I guess if you don't love books that's not very helpful), and for my kids it's tantamount to a going-out-of-business sale at the local candy store. I'm a cracked vessel constantly waiting to be filled up. Arms and eyes open wide to all around me, I find my world full of teachable, memorable, beautiful moments. It's taken me a while to understand this well.

For the past twenty-five years I've lived and moved within several different traditions; I have "indwelt" a variety of trades, crafts and communities and acquired a different skill set in each. Indwelling is about digesting the world we inhabit from the inside out. As Drusilla Scott has reminded us in *Everyman Revived*, knowledge that has not been digested in this way is inert. She writes, "We shall remain blind in theory to all that truly matters in the world so long as we do not accept indwelling as a legitimate form of knowledge."[1] Only by living inside of something, incorporating it in a tacit way – a way that goes beyond what we can say to become embedded in our way of being – can we begin to use it as knowledge that has real substantive meaning and engages us in practical action. We know through our bodies: we live bodily in a tradition and thereby indwell it. We breathe it, think about it and start to behave based on the traditional and tacit components embodied in it. It is an act of integration of mind and body, holistic and comprehensive in its tone and scope. Consider, for example, the subtle and complex forms of bodily knowledge one employs in riding a skateboard. To ride well one must indwell all of skateboarding's tacit particulars, and one does so by a continual process of experiencing, digesting, incorporating and acting on them.

I am a licensed electrician and have served an 8500-hour apprenticeship. I am also a sleight-of-hand magician and have been studying with numerous professionals from around the world for many years now. Each new outlook, idea and approach informs the way I interact with and in the world. I have been thrown into new traditions, each of which has a particular way of seeing the world and therefore of interacting with it, and as I move within these frameworks I develop ways of seeing and make them my own. I have been privy to customs, practices and skills that can be transmitted only through relationship. Apprenticeships are profound give-and-take relationships grounded in human knowing; in short, they are relational acts. They are human, interactive events founded on trust, wisdom and generosity, and their purpose is to engage and inform the other on a practical and conceptual level.

By definition, an apprentice is someone who has committed to learning a trade, craft, art or profession over an extended period of time in a personal relationship with one or more masters. These masters act as teachers, mentors and guides as knowledge is passed on from one to the other. The focus is on learning and indwelling a specific set of skills, details and duties, each of which will be communicated through a reciprocal relationship with someone who has been employed with the sole purpose of instruction.[2] It is an understanding that is situated within many layers of context, action and practice.

The way an apprentice graduates from one "term" (or level) to another is by acquiring skills and practices that enable her to do specified tasks correctly and effectively. In most trades this is formally correlated with serving X number of hours in a particular field. How is it possible, though, to quantify the knowledge acquired in a relationship of this kind? How does one really know that it is time to graduate from one term to the next?

I am reminded of my first morning on the job as an electrician's apprentice. There was much to learn. I had passed an aptitude test and was accepted into the International Brotherhood of Electrical Workers as a first-term apprentice. My foreman and soon-to-be mentor handed me a few pieces of material, including several octagon boxes, some wire and some connectors. He asked that I mount them to a concrete wall and insert the wire, commonly called BX in the industry, into a few small connectors often referred to as L-16s. I had no idea what I was doing, and began to experiment with what would eventually become a simple, everyday task. When the time came for the foreman to inspect my work, he looked at what I had accomplished and smiled, then began to critique, question and mildly ridicule my attempt and my lack of skill. I was crushed – and so was the wire, for in my haste and enthusiasm to complete the job, I had twisted the connectors so tight that I had flattened and cracked the cable, permanently damaging it. I had wasted time, material and energy. Within a few humbling minutes, I realized how many more of these experiences I was going to have to endure. For the next 8500 hours I would learn much about how to do one thing and not another. I would work towards becoming an electrician by doing, by practising and by indwelling[3] the very tradition I was now a part of.

This is an essay about knowledge of a particular kind: that of the tacit dimension. Scientist and philosopher Michael Polanyi coined the phrase *tacit knowledge* in the late 1950s. His primary concern can be understood as the question: What precisely is reliable knowledge? Polanyi believed, from his experience in the academic community, that science and philosophy had become preoccupied with the notion of knowledge as something detached, neutral and disinterested; the idea of knowledge based on personal belief had been tossed aside. This detached, objective approach, usually applied to the exact sciences, he believed to be mistaken and a false ideal.

"Tacit," for Polanyi, is not quite the same as what is commonly referred to as "implicit." The tacit dimension is not just a set of implicit actions or an implicit set of functional terms. It is the structure and formulation of knowledge bearing out the claim that "...we can know more than we can tell."[4] It refers to the fact that much knowledge not only *is not* put into words, but *cannot be* put into words: we may know about "A" without being able to articulate exactly what we know about "A." It is often the case that one can know certain things only in practice and not just as explicit objects.

Polanyi believes that *all* acts of knowing, in fact, are rooted in and tend to rely on inexpressible or inarticulate operations of the mind. These operations situate the knower and the known together in a close relationship of being, and are grounded in what he calls "subsidiary" and "focal" awareness. The engaged, active knower participates in both types of awareness and integrates them into a larger whole. This is the basic structure of tacit knowing — which, according to Polanyi, provides the unifying ground for all knowledge. Tacit knowing is knowledge, but it is knowledge of a particular sort that goes beyond what we can tell. For Polanyi there is nothing second-rate about this kind of knowing; it may be limited, but it is indeed knowledge. The tacit aspect of any act of knowing is grounded in the embodied action of *practice*. We "attend from" the particulars – that is, we do not focus on them but use them as necessary background to focus on the whole. The particulars are subsidiary. If we know how to ride a bike, for example, we do not focus on the particulars involved in the action of riding a bike; we simply ride it, but in doing so we are incorporating innumerable particulars. If we were to attend to or focus on those particulars, we would not in fact be riding the bike at all. The explicit action of riding the bike is facilitated by an interaction between the subsidiary and focal aspects of the tacit dimension.

Tacit knowing and inarticulate knowledge are related, but are not necessarily the same thing. Polanyi claims that there are elements of the tacit dimension that are inarticulable. Perhaps the best example of this is the act of recognizing a face. There are aspects of this experience that can be spoken of explicitly, but clearly much of the way we know a face must remain inarticulable. We know the face tacitly. It is only by relying on many inexpressible clues that we can recognize one face over another. But the act of knowing something tacitly is defined not only negatively but positively: more than mere inexpression, to know something tacitly is a matter of indwelling the particulars, "attending from" these clues to focus on a meaningful whole. I may, for example, have explicit knowledge of certain mathematical formulae. I may indeed possess true and justified belief in them. However, I must rely on many other complex particulars that I have come to assume from within the mathematical tradition. It is these particulars that enable me to use and work with the formulae.

The tacit knowledge required to pick up a glass of liquid and have it reach the mouth each time may not be as detailed and layered as the action of a sea captain docking a 78,000-ton cruise ship, but both require aspects of the tacit dimension. Both access tacit particulars, but each operates on a different level of focal and subsidiary awareness. Similarly, hammering a nail is not as tacitly complex as playing the piano, but both rely on tacit particulars that are not in focus. As Polanyi explains, if the pianist shifts her attention from the piece that she is playing to what her fingers are doing with the keys, she may get confused and have to stop playing altogether. She must attend *from* one thing in order to accomplish another that she is attending *to*: her fingers must operate tacitly in relation to the keyboard as her attention is focused on playing the piece. The pianist has a subsidiary awareness of the keys and pedals, her fingers and feet, and the piano, and a focal awareness of playing the piece. Through experience and practice she acquires a tacit knowledge of playing the piano that she can proximally attend from in order to perform a piece. It is conceivable, theoretically, that one could articulate at least some of the tacit particulars involved in playing the piano; however, in order to play the piece as a finished whole the pianist must never attend to those particulars, but must indwell them. She must integrate a skill set of unspecifiable particulars that merge in a relationship between the pianist and the keyboard, and it is through practice that she comes to know how to do this. In fact, there is a direct relationship between the performative skill of the pianist and the level of tacit knowledge she has acquired: the greater the tacit content of one's subsidiary awareness, the greater the focal ability. This relationship is essential for disciplines of all kinds, including formal reasoning. Explicit thought, articulate knowing and communication all rely on tacit knowing. As Marjorie Grene has pointed out, what is fundamental to understanding tacit knowing is the relationship of the subsidiary and focal aspects of the tacit dimension.[5] The important thing is not just that the tacit dimension exists, but *how the tacit relates to the explicit.*

Polanyi states at the outset of his book *Personal Knowledge* that it is a work primarily interested in the justification of knowledge. The question of how knowledge is justified is one about which there is considerable disagreement among philosophers, but one of the more dominant approaches is that of foundationalism. Descartes is a foundationalist; that is, he insists that all beliefs must have a starting point or foundation. His system of thought sought to eradicate any idea or presupposition that was not certain, and the one thing he regarded as indubitably certain was that thinking itself necessarily implies the existence of a consciousness. It is here that he begins. Doubting everything, he argued that he could start over with no assumptions other than his own existence. Nevertheless, ironically, his position with respect to the justification of knowledge rests on earlier claims that cannot be justified. The statements of mathematics he considers innate and self-evident and therefore certain; they are foundational claims that need no justification.

One of the weaknesses of the foundationalist claim to knowledge is that of the infinite regress. In order to doubt one thing, one must believe another. Each belief is justified to the extent to which one can accept and believe earlier ideas on which it rests; however, each belief resting on another claim becomes more difficult, if not impossible, to verify and justify. According to Michael Polanyi, the tacit dimension provides the unifying ground for all knowledge and addresses to some degree the infinite regress of the foundationalist position. He admits that the notion of a "personal" type of "knowledge" is paradoxical. He sets out to establish and hold on to an alternative ideal for knowledge, opposed to the intellectual prejudice that asserts only universal, detached and objective empirical claims. For Polanyi the tacit and personal component of the knowing subject can and does accurately account for average, everyday experience. The apparent contradiction is resolved by modifying one's conception of knowing to include a comprehensive account of the tacit dimension.[6] Through this model Polanyi is careful to avoid the trap of radical subjectivism, claiming that his approach is not one that spirals downward into moral and ethical obscurantism. As Richard Gelwick argues, "Polanyi deeply believes in objectivity, but of a different kind and on a different basis from what is widely understood."[7]

One reason for my interest in Polanyi's work is that I believe the academic community has ignored his notion of the tacit dimension for too long.[8] In that community the widely accepted Cartesian model continues to dwarf Polanyi's notion; as Charles Taylor suggests, Descartes' hold on the tradition of philosophy runs deep:

Descartes is not in fashion these days. He is rejected as a dualist, as too rationalist, as clinging to an outmoded psychology, and for many other reasons. Yet even though his terms are repudiated, we frequently find the basic structure remaining in place.[9]

This "basic structure," Taylor suggests, is still very much a part of the modern mind. Its influence is significant, and because of what he calls its "framework status" it is rarely consciously focused on; rather, it is simply taken for granted and therefore often shapes what occurs on a conscious or, as Polanyi would call it, a focal level.

In contrast, much of his work has been picked up by the theological community in an attempt to lend weight to the fiduciary element found in all theo-metaphysical claims. It is for this second reason that I believe his thinking has often been ignored. I wonder to what degree other thinkers have casually disregarded Polanyi's work precisely because theists have sometimes harboured him as their champion as they seek to justify their faithful claims.

Polanyi's work advocates a serious change from some aspects of presently accepted modes of thought. His work has been called difficult; without question it is controversial and perhaps not always well understood.[10] At the same time he has also been praised as one of the greatest scientist-philosophers of our century. He has unlocked a philosophical door that I believe needs to be permanently kept open. Tacit knowledge, comprising practical and applicable knowledge acquired in the form of skills, in a shared community of tradition[11] and in relationship to others, is a valid and essential way of understanding and apprehending the world we inhabit.

I would like to call your attention to two examples from two of my favourite philosophers: one from the life of Socrates, the other from Pascal. At the trial before his death, Socrates engages in a dialogue with his accusers. He reprimands those who he believes are not "in the know" and defends himself by showing that he is wise, having taken the time and made the effort to find those that are worldly and knowledgeable.[12] In the *Apology* he speaks of the people he has met on his philosophical journey in search of someone who truly "knows"; he talks to politicians, leaders, poets and others reputed to be wise, but is continually disappointed. He states, "...those with the best reputations seemed to me nearly the most deficient, in my investigation in accordance with the god...

for they too say many noble things, but they know nothing of what they speak."[13] Socrates is disillusioned by the so-called wise men; he finds they actually know very little. However, the final group he examines are the manual artisans, the craftsmen. These are people with knowledge rooted in practice: to know a craft is to practise and do a craft. Socrates tells us that "...they did have knowledge of things which I did not have knowledge of, and in this way they were wiser than I."[14] He recognizes the legitimacy of the tradespeople's knowledge, and even though he goes on to say that the artisans too were misguided, he does offer them a degree of respect and support that the others did not warrant. This first example sheds some light on the importance of practice and on the skill-like nature of knowledge.

Pascal invented the *machine d'arithmétique,* better known as the Pascaline, while working with his father from 1642 to 1644. The device resembled the mechanical calculator of the early 1940s and was intended to aid in the tedious calculations involved in the tax work Pascal and his father did. Working closely with a local craftsman, Pascal went through fifty models before developing a machine that would work. Each model was built on the understanding gained through the previous one, and over the course of this process the mechanics of the device were improved on and many ineffectual ideas discarded. He finally arrived at a finished working calculator that could be patented; it was a complicated apparatus involving many precisely cut gears and small-machined metal pieces.[15] This second example points to the cumulative effect and the skill-like nature of the tacit dimension. Each lesson learned was a result of new and practical hands-on knowledge gained by experience, by trial and error – a process that enabled the recognition of the need for an extra screw, a simple tweak or a finely machined metal piece. Pascal and his craftsman were involved in an apprenticeship of a particular sort, each informing the other as they sought to perfect their new invention. It took them two years and fifty models to get it right.

While this elbow knowledge is transmitted from journeyman to apprentice, important things are happening – things that have implications for what we know and how we move, live and love. The subtleties and nuances of this give-and-take relationship provide the unifying ground for all knowledge.

THE ROOTS GO DEEP

"Man is in the world and only in the world does he know himself." —Maurice Merleau-Ponty

Knowledge comes through practice and not merely through textual or propositional accounts. Book knowledge is important, but it is not the only kind. Arguing for tacit knowing in a culture that has many of its philosophical roots beginning in the rationalistic movement of the seventeenth century poses some serious challenges. The emphasis on rules, precepts and knowledge-as-universals is inconsistent with the notion of tacit knowing. Polanyi is concerned not primarily with universals, but with particulars and how they relate to universals. This is one of the problems of an essay concerned with tacit knowledge. How does one make something propositionally explicit and yet claim it is a tacitly held notion at the same time? Explicit knowledge is typically viewed as objective knowledge; it is impersonal and supposed to be demonstrable. Tacit knowledge by definition is not. If tacit knowing cannot be articulated in an explicit manner, then how then can we analyze it in any way? Tacit knowing is like the forest that cannot be seen for the trees. Polanyi refers to the paradoxical example in Poe's *The Purloined Letter*, of that "momentous document lying casually in front of everybody, and hence overlooked by all."[16]

Polanyi writes a detailed and explicit analysis of personal knowledge in *The Tacit Dimension*. He suggests that we reconsider human knowledge by starting with the fact that "we can know more than we can tell."[17] This statement is significant for some and frustrating for others; I can imagine many philosophers not getting very far beyond his short opening and concise phrase. Why, and how, does one write, speak and tell of that which is unspeakable? If it cannot be spoken of, then doesn't the simple statement of that fact already constitute everything that can be said about it? To suggest that I will talk of things that I can't talk about seems to be a philosophical contradiction. And yet this statement, for all of its potential obscurity, may shine a light on our experience. Tacit knowing has been considered by many to be a meaningless category because of the lack of precision surrounding its definition. However, when philosophers argue that tacit knowing is not knowing because it cannot be expressed in words, they are assuming that other types of knowledge can be articulated.

I believe that reputable knowledge is to be found in the practice of any discipline, and that practice is a warranted path towards knowing. Practice is simply *doing*: to practise medicine is to *do* medicine. To practice cooking is to be meaningfully engaged in the *action* of cooking. In order to practise any discipline or skill, one must behave in a particular way, adhere to specific (but not *specified*) rules and incorporate past experience in one's actions. For example, I can speak of being an electrician in terms of propositional knowledge; I may know of electrical theories and I may be able to articulate the dangers of working on live electrical circuits. However, until I have practised or until I have been involved in the doing of electrical work I cannot practically speak of this trade in a relevant and useful manner. It is the synthesis of theory and practice that makes for a good electrician.

I remember winning a high school nail-hitting contest, the Heatherbrae Hammer Heavy Hitting Contest. I was a Grade 8 weakling who had yoyo skills, rode a skateboard and had very few cool friends. But I won out over the big boys, the jocks and those who could have taken me in a fistfight in a matter of minutes, and I believe it had to do with my tacit skills in using a hammer. The contest was to see who could hit a nail into a tree trunk the fastest. I didn't need strength, because I had precision: I rarely missed the head of the nail. The muscle t-shirts, on the other hand, missed it often. They had strength, but I had practice. My uncle had taught me how to use a hammer properly – bend at the elbow, not the shoulder, and focus on the nail head – and I had discovered how to execute this instruction by actually doing it countless times. Many contestants lost to my prowess with a hammer that week. I made it into the newspaper. Cool. The jocks still managed to attract the girls, though; I wonder why.

My uncle was able to articulate something about hammering a nail, but most of what was involved in that skill could only be acquired tacitly by practice. Polanyi tells us that a skilful performance is achieved by observing a set of rules which may not be known as such by the person following them. The principles that keep a cyclist balanced, for example, are not specifically known by the cyclist. A scientist could draw up the mathematical and geometric relationships between road and cyclist; graphs could be generated and formulas dictated as to how the bicyclist might remain upright at all times. However, this attempted formulation of the methodology behind the riding of a bike would be meaningless to a six-year-old learning how to ride a bike for the first time, and equally meaningless to him a year later when he had mastered the skill. It is only by relying on an unspecifiable set of particulars that the youngster is able to ride the bike. These specific (but unspecified) bike-riding particulars are an instance of the subsidiary aspect of Polanyi's two-tiered theory of tacit knowing. The particulars involved in maintaining balance are a kind of knowledge that cannot be explicitly justified, yet they are genuine knowledge in that they enable the cyclist to make contact with reality in a meaningful way: when he "attends from" (or works from) these particulars, the action of bike riding follows.

Moreover, the more the cyclist engages in cycling, the more thorough his knowledge of these particulars becomes. The same is true in any discipline, including science. As Polanyi accurately claims, "Science is operated by the skill of the scientist and it is through the exercise of his skill that he shapes his scientific knowledge."[18] Like the cyclist who develops skill through riding and the mathematician who learns theory through practice, the scientist can acquire knowledge by practising its application: the greater one's practical ability, the greater one's knowledge. Polanyi writes:

> We are relying on our awareness of a combination of muscular acts for attending to the performance of a skill. We are attending *from* these elementary movements *to* the achievement of their joint purpose, and hence are usually unable to specify these elementary acts. We may call this the *functional structure* of tacit knowing.[19]

Modernity has been interested in the answer, the solution, strict definition and explicit knowledge claims, and as a result, other avenues to knowledge have often been ignored. Drusilla Scott speaks to the level of tacit unawareness with respect to knowledge claims that lack any explicit definition. These ways of knowing are denied, or at least challenged, by the frameworks, the assumptions and even the language of the philosopher and scientist. Scott writes:

> There are examples everywhere of the use of 'science' to undermine confidence in any other way of knowing. "More research is needed" – "Statistics tell us" – "Laboratory tests have conclusively proved" – this kind of phrase is common and builds up the assumption that if you don't know in a scientific way, you don't know. Any judgement of value, any intuitive wisdom, is banished to the realm of fantasy or whim, while any statistical or scientific type of statement gets an automatic endorsement.[20]

The worldview or framework in which we operate in everyday life is informed implicitly and explicitly on many levels. The framework helps us make sense of our experience and is also self-perpetuating in that it tacitly informs and supports itself. Personal knowledge influences even the simplest of habitual tasks. Polanyi writes, "Even the most strictly mechanized procedure leaves something to personal skill in the exercise of which an individual bias may enter."[21] The moment we start to file sense experiences cognitively, the tacit dimension begins to water its root – a root grounded in a type of knowledge that is always personal. This act of fertilization of sense experience is a result of our being thrown into a world not of our own making. The acquisition of explicit knowledge is not merely an apprehension of sense experiences viewed in an empirical manner. Tacit knowledge is the root. As Polanyi has written, "While tacit knowledge can be possessed by itself, explicit knowledge must rely on being tacitly understood and applied."[22]

Jerry Gill suggests that it is ultimately misleading to call this starting point a "foundation." In support of Polanyi's thesis regarding the tacit component of all knowledge, he argues for regarding it as an "axis" rather than a foundation. This image of an axis, he believes, avoids the problem of infinite regress as it suggests an anchoring that is not fixed and not in need of further support. The main point here is that the centre of all knowing resides within embodied tacit activity.[23]

A DEFINITION

The word "tacit," from Latin *tacite*, meaning unspoken or silent, is most often used to describe a notion or feeling that is not expressed in an explicit way but could be; in other words, to describe that which is merely implicit. Many different writers and thinkers have made use of some notion of the tacit. Consider the French philosopher Blaise Pascal's concept of emotional intelligence, recognized in the often-quoted saying, "The heart has its reasons that reason cannot know." It was precisely this duality of instinct and discourse that formed the basis for Pascal's resistance to the sovereignty of reason.[24] Instinct in humans was synonymous with intuitive knowledge, and Pascal often referred to this intuition as the knowledge of the heart, an inarticulate, emotional and non-rational (though not irrational) knowledge. But this is not what Polanyi means by "tacit." Nor does the standard dictionary definition of the word give us many clues as to what Polanyi had in mind; it defines "tacit" as describing actions that are not openly expressed or stated, but implied, understood or inferred. Consider the use of the word in this recent excerpt from an editorial in the *New York Times*, March 10, 2005, entitled "Death Behind Bars":

> Many publicly run systems, which provide most of the care for the nation's inmates, are equally bad. The root problem is that the country has tacitly decided to starve the prison system of medical care, even though AIDS, tuberculosis and hepatitis are rampant behind bars.

In this instance, "tacit" describes a decision that is made in just the same way that any other decision is made, with the sole qualification that it is not stated openly; it could be, but it isn't. Although this is common usage, it is not what Polanyi meant by "tacit." The tacit knowledge he speaks of does operate on an implicit level, but to define it as merely "implicit" is an oversimplification because it does not address the crucial distinction between the subsidiary and focal aspects.

It is also inaccurate to identify Polanyi's tacit dimension as involving unconscious, subconscious or pre-conscious activity. For example, when writing with a pen and paper we are fully aware of the pen and paper we are using; we rely on them only in a subsidiary manner, but we are not unconscious of them. He writes, "The clues of tacit knowing and the elements of tacit performing are usually difficult to identify and sometimes they are quite unspecifiable… but all this does not make a subsidiary state an unconscious one."[25]

Polanyi maintains that the acquisition of language, as understood by Noam Chomsky, is also a tacit performance. He suggests that Chomsky's notion of "…intricate chains of unconscious quasi-inferential steps"[26] used in the acquisition of language are related to the tacit dimension. Chomsky calls this intellectual component a language acquisition device, and Polanyi refers to it as subsidiary knowledge and to its application as a tacit integration or a tacit operation. He writes,

> The ideal of a strictly explicit knowledge is indeed self-contra-dictory; deprived of their tacit coefficients, all spoken words, all formulae, all maps and graphs are strictly meaningless. An exact mathematical theory means nothing unless we recognize an inexact non-mathematical knowledge on which it bears and a person whose judgment upholds this bearing.[27]

Similarly, if, when using language, we were to switch our attention to the formal terms set out explicitly in Chomksy's generative grammar, we would ultimately deprive them of their capacity to generate meaning. The rules work well when we attend from them in a subsidiary manner. They act as a tacit guide when speaking, writing and listening to the spoken word.

Heinz Otto Sibum writes of gestural knowledge in terms of the "actor's performance of work" and how it may change according to a specific circumstance, skill or approach to technology. In an attempt to replicate an experiment of the nineteenth century, he acknowledges the challenges and difficulties surrounding such duplication. He speaks, for example, of a specific thermometer used during the original experiment, and admits that rebuilding a similar tool may not be possible due to insufficient information and skill. He also speaks of the necessity of the scientist's ability and refers to the activity involved as an "artistic mechanical per-formance." Sibum is acknowledging the role played by accumulated background knowledge and experience with regard to accurate experimental replication. He is, in short, arguing for the tacit dimension. Without actually specifying in detail the traditional and apprentice-like nature and transference of tacit knowledge, he speaks of a form of knowledge being passed on from one to another, a process that depends on acts of personal communication and/or the imitation of others. He admits that personal experience was in fact necessary for the replication to succeed.

> It is well known that doing an experiment is not only determined by material culture but also by the actor's abilities to interact properly with the objects and each other. A range of terms such as skill [and] tacit knowledge…are used to draw our attention to this crucial aspect of human practices.[28]

To illustrate yet again the distinction between "tacit" meaning simply "implicit" and "tacit" as Polanyi understands the term: there is a tacit acceptance, in the West, of the notion that democracy is the best form of government. In most political conversations one proceeds on the assumption that policies or solutions are to be implemented in a democratic way. It is not something that needs to be made explicit in all writing and conversations. On the surface, this form of tacit understanding is a given: all human interaction, however inconsequential, must involve some forms of tacit apprehension of this or that. But this notion of "tacit" is almost trivial. What is of importance, for Polanyi's notion of the tacit dimension, is the relationship of tacit knowing to practice. As Marjorie Grene states, "What matters is not that there is something unspecifiable, for example, in science, but how unspecifiability works and what it accomplishes."[29] In other words, it is not that the mere existence of the tacit that is important, but *how, in actual practice, it relates to the explicit.*

All actions are informed by and through the particulars that make up tacit knowledge. A few years ago I was diagnosed with a medical condition known as Morton's Neuroma, an orthopaedic problem that manifests itself through inflammation of several joints in the feet. It took several years to get a proper diagnosis. What is of significance is not only the length of time it took, but more specifically how the diagnosis eventually made itself known. After visiting many doctors and having my x-rays examined, I found my condition escalating and still undiagnosed. I ignored the problem for several years until I found myself walking next to a former physiotherapist who was interested in the limp that I had developed. He had me remove my shoes, pull off my socks and raise my pant legs, only to declare almost immediately, "You have Morton's Neuroma." Surprised at having visited many doctors and specialists without ever hearing the term, I began my research. A few months later I was given the formal, medical and orthopaedic diagnosis of Morton's Neuroma.

This physiotherapist and friend of mine had a clear, precise and tacit knowledge born of specific experiences that allowed him to recognize my physical problem immediately. What he knew about feet and about my feet in particular was determined by his history, the physiotherapeutic tradition with which he had interacted over time and his personal experiences and practice. It was brought to bear without articulation either to me or to himself in his own head. In an embodied, practical way, it was his experience working out what his experience had worked in. Polanyi speaks of similar examples. The piano player, the child riding the bicycle and the carpenter hammering a nail all make use of tacit knowledge.

Here again the particulars of a skill appear to be unspecifiable, but this time not in the sense of our being ignorant of them. For in this case we can ascertain the details of our performance quite well, and its unspecifiability consists in the fact that the performance is paralyzed if we focus our attention on these details.[30]

Glasses sitting on a shelf or hanging from a rack will always be seen as a detached and impersonal object with a specific function to serve. Remove the glasses from the shelf, put them on, and you will say, "Yes, I'm wearing glasses." There may even be a slight shock of recognition as your eyes adjust. The glasses cover your eyes and act as a filter for every ray of light that makes its way to your retina. In short, they become an extension of your eyes. And they will always colour and affect the way you see the world; your outlook has now been altered. However, once the glasses are no longer viewed as an instrument or object – once the object has become a part of the subject – the glasses situate themselves within the tacit dimension. They assume a tacit position in the sense that they are no longer recognized explicitly as an object and yet they continue to affect the focal awareness of the subject wearing them. As Polanyi would maintain, the glasses are subsidiarily informing and imposing on the focal activity of the subject. Tacit knowledge has replaced any tactile sense or recognition of the object in and of itself: they are no longer glasses in the same sense as when they were sitting on the table or in a case. We know the role they are playing as they correct our vision, and at the same time we don't know that we know it.

Gilbert Ryle, in his essay "Knowing How and Knowing That," speaks of the role that implicit rules and regulations play with respect to skilful knowledge. He suggests that their function is similar to the effect of wearing glasses. He writes, "We look through them but not at them. And as a person who looks much at his spectacles betrays that he has difficulties in looking through them, so people who appeal much to principles show that they do not know how to act."[31] Polanyi clarifies this example with reference to the classic case of a subject wearing a pair of spectacles that make the world appear upside down. In his essay "Vision without Inversion of the Retinal Image," G. M. Stratton writes of an experiment in which he wore such glasses for an extended period of time and after eight days was able to overcome the change in his vision.[32] As Polanyi points out, for over half a century the results were universally misinterpreted as the mere reversal of the inverted image, but further experimentation has shown that the visual image remains inverted; as suggested by the observations of F. W. Snyder and N. H. Pronko in their essay "Vision without Spatial Inversion," the subject learns to respond appropriately to what is falsely seen as inverted images, and so to move around successfully in the world in spite of them.[33] Polanyi writes, "The subject gets to find his way around because he has acquired a new way of seeing things, which appropriately coordinates his inverted vision with his muscular feeling, his sense of balance and his hearing."[34]

This act of reintegration is what is important. It is not through explicit directions that the subject is able to reorient herself and behave effectively, Polanyi suggests, but rather the exact opposite. Explicit rules for interpreting the images (what is right side up is really upside down, what is left is really right, and so on) *hinder* reintegration. Nor is reintegration a spontaneous reaction to the lenses; rather, it occurs as a result of protracted and sometimes strenuous effort. It is by and through practice that this act of reintegration takes place. The subject tries to see properly and achieves success only through sustained practical effort, whereupon correct seeing begins to take place without conscious effort.

> We must conclude then it is the effort of our imagination, seeking to reinterpret our vision in a way that will control the scene before us, which produces the right way of seeing inverted images. This is the dynamics of tacit knowing: the questing imagination vaguely anticipating experiences not yet grounded in subsidiary particulars evokes these subsidiaries and thus implements the experience the imagination has sought to achieve.[35]

According to Polanyi, once the subsidiary particulars involved in the action of tacit knowing are established, one shifts one's attention to them only at the cost of losing the overall meaning of the action. In other words, the less aware we are of those particulars, the more focused we will be on seeing, and on what it is we are seeing.

Tacit knowing speaks of the relationship between the subsidiary and focal, or distal and proximal (two other terms for the same thing), aspects of all practical *from-to* knowing. By relying on our awareness of one term (the subsidiary or proximal) we can attend to another term (the focal or distal). We attend *from* something in order that we might focus on something else. We use our body without being explicitly aware of it in order that we might attend to things beyond our physical or embodied selves.

> We attend from something for attending to something else; namely from the first term to the second term of the tacit relation. Using the language of anatomy, we may call the first term proximal, and the second term distal. It is the proximal term, then, of which we have a knowledge that we cannot tell.[36]

In other words, the "first term" of tacit knowing, the particulars from which we are attending, is "near" to us, while the "second term," the thing on which we are focused, is "far" from us. This, Polanyi claims, is the functional structure of tacit knowing.

> It is not surprising, therefore, that we may often apprehend wholes without ever having focally attended to their particulars. In such cases we are actually ignorant, or perhaps more precisely speaking, focally ignorant of these particulars: we know them only subsidiarily in terms of what they jointly mean, but cannot tell what they are in themselves. Practical skills and practical experience contain much more information than people possessing this expert knowledge can ever tell. Particulars that are not known focally are unspecifiable, and there are vast domains of knowledge, relating to living things, the particulars of which are largely unspecifiable.[37]

This type of knowing, especially among members of a community, is deeply affected by hundreds of years of history, culture, technique and tradition. I will show, in the next section, that the world of sleight-of-hand magic has much to offer with respect to our understanding of not only *what* we know, but more importantly *how* we know.

THE "CUPS AND BALLS" AND THE TACIT ROLE OF PRACTICE

The trick known as "Cups and Balls" has been performed for hundreds of years and is considered to be a classic in magic. It's a technical sleight-of-hand piece found deep within the craft and is probably familiar to most people who have ever seen a magic show. Its closest cousin is the three-shell game, often played on the streets of major cities around the world. Local con artists will attempt to win your money as you guess which shell has the nomadic pea under it. Like the three-shell game, the Cups and Balls uses three cups, but differs in that it uses three balls instead of one. Its relationship to the three-shell game is only superficial, as the one is an attempt to confuse so as to win money while the other is performed as a piece of pure and simple sleight of hand. It is and has been for years considered the litmus test of the working magician. The tacit dimension brings itself to bear on each performer in a different way, as tacit constituents depend on the tradition and cultural context in which they are situated.

Professor Hoffmann wrote of the Cups and Balls, "It is the groundwork of all legerdemain."[38] Many scholars of the craft agree. The trick was first discussed by a Roman philosopher and dramatist, Seneca the Younger, when he wrote of the jugglers' "cups and pebbles" sometime around 50 CE.[39] This is the earliest undisputed reference to this particular piece of magic. In 1404 Joseph of Ulm represented it in his coloured drawing, "Children of the Planets: Luna."[40] The literary groundwork for it, however, was established in Reginald Scot's *Discovery of Witchcraft* in 1584.[41] It's here that we find the first detailed description of the workings behind the effect, and drawings of the preferred types of cups in use by the magicians of the day. Bob Read, a historian of magic, suggests that the history of the *escamoteur* (cups-and-balls conjuror) was very much a part not only of French culture and history but more specifically of the political conversation of the eighteenth and nineteenth century. He writes, "[T]hroughout the eighteenth and at least the first half of the nineteenth century the escamoteur was in every sense a part of the uniquely French landscape."[42]

The Cups and Balls is a piece of sleight-of-hand magic that requires much skill and a profound sense of showmanship and ability to misdirect. What's so interesting about this particular piece of magic is the number of different elements the magician must rely on in order to perform it well. It draws on many different disciplines of the magician in order to communicate to the spectator that a genuine piece of magic is occurring. The tacit informs the explicit and plays a significant role in the performance of the piece, as we shall see.

The effect is based on the "vanish," the transposition and reproduction of small balls under a set of metal or wooden cups. A ball will vanish from under one cup and appear under another. A ball will penetrate one cup to be found resting on another. A ball placed into the magician's hands will instantly be found under one of the cups. Hoffmann explains:

> The whole art of cup and ball conjuring resolves itself into two elements. The exhibition of a ball under a cup where a moment previously there was nothing; and the disappearance of a ball from beneath a cup under which the audience have just seen it placed.[43]

When a ball vanishes from one hand and appears under a cup, the spectator may say, "It must be sleight of hand." In other words, some mechanical function that escapes detection is producing the desired effect; even though the spectator may be aware that the magician is applying a certain kind of knowledge and skill, the underlying tacit particulars that the magician attends from will remain hidden. And as with the pianist, these particulars that inform or guide the sleight of hand are a crucial aspect of the tacit dimension and are not susceptible of articulation. The knowledge required to perform this piece well can never be taken merely from the textbook definition of the vanish itself; the ball is not just "placed into the hand" as any other object might be, but placed in a particular way that defies verbal description. If one were to attempt the action based only on the written instruction without other tacit particulars, the result would be less than a vanish. The magician must adhere to other tacit impositions that will become part of his knowledge only through embodied experience by way of committed, long-term practice, refining the movements involved until the technical aspects become subsidiary tacit points of reference. Once established in this way, they blend together to make up the final effect of the vanish. As David Devant and Nevil Maskelyne write in *Our Magic*, it is via a series of combined processes that a given result is produced. This idea of a combination of processes, subtle and intricate but unspecified, points to the more refined distinction of Polanyi's notion of subsidiary and focal awareness. It's an interplay of little things – one tiny act depending on the other – that brings about the intended outcome. Devant and Maskelyne write:

> In a like manner, every magical operation may be subjected to a specific technical analysis, and thereby a clearer understanding may be gained of its true nature and position in the general theory of magic. Of course, not every result attainable by magical processes is so simple as the foregoing in its genesis. Some results are due to a combination of processes, each of which has its own separate origin. But, however simple or however complex may be the operations concerned in producing a given result, their source or sources can be traced quite readily.[44]

This process for the magician would involve attending from the subsidiary aspects of the mechanical nature of the vanish proper, the significant particulars that make up each movement or motion within the workings of the specific sleight. It is only by attending from the particulars in this subsidiary manner that the vanish can be performed. They are like tacit pieces of a puzzle brought together to form the comprehensive whole, the effect itself, which Polanyi would call the focal point.

Perhaps a detailed quote from *Modern Magic* will help to illustrate the point. The passage below is an attempt by Hoffmann to explain a visual and magical experience. However, what is written on the page only marginally reflects what actually occurs. This is what the audience will supposedly see – the explicit actions that make up the Cups and Balls. They are not the mechanical functions that are hidden from the spectator and tacitly adhered to by the magician in the performance of each and every sleight.

> A ball is taken in the right hand, transferred to the left, and thence ordered to pass under the cup. The hand is opened; the ball has vanished, and, on the cup being lifted, is found beneath it. Again, the ball, first exhibited in the right hand, is thence openly transferred, either directly under the cup, or first to the left hand, and thence to the cup. All having seen it placed beneath the cup, it is now commanded to depart, and on again lifting the cup, it is found to have vanished. It will hardly be believed, until proved by experiment, of what numerous and surprising combinations these simple elements are capable.[45]

The words describe what is taking place at a focal level. They describe the effect achieved by the magician and seen by the spectator as a meaningful whole – that of a ball being placed from one hand into another and then vanishing. This is precisely what

Polanyi is referring to when he speaks of focal awareness. The spectator is focally aware of the action of a ball being placed from one hand into the other. The magician's focal attention, however, is on the vanish.

Now let's look at a textual description of what is occurring from a sleight-of-hand perspective. The words attempt to describe all the little actions of the performer, actions that are not seen by the spectator and not focused on by the performer. Edwin Sachs writes:

> The very first thing the learner must acquire is the knack of slipping the ball rapidly from the exposed view to the concealed position in a secure manner. The ball is partly slid, partly rolled, partly dropped into the position, the thumb, with a slight motion (which in time will become quite an unconscious one) pressing it finally home.[46]

Although the description gives us more information about what is happening, it is only an approximation, for this partial sliding, rolling and dropping motion performed by the magician cannot actually be detailed in words. Practice, which focuses on achieving the sleight itself, will determine exactly how and when these actions are applied. Practice will determine what it means to "slide, roll and drop" the ball, exactly how to move the fingers, the arms and the body. The embodied acquisition of each element of this knowledge will occur tacitly as the magician continues to work out the sleight, and in the course of this process it must move beyond the mere propositional account. Focusing on the individually articulated steps will interfere with the performance. "Rules of art can be useful," writes Polanyi, "but they do not determine the practice of an art; they are maxims, which can serve as a guide to an art only if they can be integrated into the practical knowledge of the art. They cannot replace this knowledge."[47]

The skill, the methodology and the tradition entailed by this sleight are described in a propositional format and yet can only be translated into action via the tacit knowledge *attended from* by the magician. All of the knowledge gained by the magician from the first time she practised a sleight, and from the moment that the sleight was learned as described in the text, comes to bear on how this particular series of movements is fused together. Without relying on these tacit particulars, the vanish could not be considered a vanish at all, because the effect would not be achieved; all that would happen would be the action of transferring a ball from one hand to the other in a strangely elaborate way. The magician must rely on tacit knowing in order for the true meaning behind the event to occur and be communicated to the spectator.

Tacit knowledge is personal partly because it is necessarily embodied knowledge, and therefore unique to the individual. The implication of the written description of movements involved in a sleight is that there is only one way to perform it. In fact, however, its actual performance by different individuals gives rise to various approaches one can take when vanishing a ball, with each performer's specific approach integrated into the whole of her experience as a magician. David Devant refers to this as a "systematising of the knowledge"[48] that a magician possesses. Polanyi would call it "indwelling." By relying on this system of tacit knowledge, an experienced magician can recreate a simple vanish of a ball by means of particulars only hinted at in a written description. A good way of illustrating this is to imagine that the text has been given to a non-magician with no prior knowledge of sleight-of-hand magic.

An magician observing the non-magician's attempt to carry it out would immediately recognize the lack of tacit knowledge as the non-magician telegraphed the key moments in the vanish of the ball. The magician with years of practice possesses the "iceberg" of integrated tacit knowledge of which the articulated description is only an explicit tip and indwells this knowledge even in following a description. With no prior tacit knowledge of sleight of hand and therefore no tacit particulars to attend from, the inexperienced person following the same description ever so carefully and smoothly does not achieve the vanish; instead, it appears to be merely a transfer of the ball from one hand to the other and remains nothing more than a demonstration of technical skill. This lack of knowledge of particulars I call a "tacit impediment."

KNOWLEDGE AS ACTION, THE BODY AND BELIEF AND INDWELLING

Knowing is intimately linked to what we do, and tacit knowledge is always transmitted in an embodied manner. It is through this personal immersion in the particulars of subsidiary and focal awareness that we can act in any given way. The knowledge that the magician acquires is something adhered to through practice. So too the arts of doing and knowing are linked together in an embodied manner of being in the world. It is through personal acts of participation that we do and know. We participate; we act based on our belief about reality and our experience of it.

Recognizing the primary role that our beliefs play in the knowledge-making process is essential to understanding the work of Polanyi. The kind of belief we are talking about entails a personal commitment. It is an act of recognition that is not a part of any explicit process of reasoning. Without this commitment, Polanyi argues, scientific knowledge would not be possible. We can only begin to know because we believe reality is imposing on us in a particular and compelling way. The commitment of the philosopher, like that of the scientist or magician, is grounded in a belief of one kind or another. The mathematician too must commit to and believe in the assumptions of geometry and accept them without absolute demonstration. It is this type of belief structure that Polanyi was trying to restore. He saw an imbalance in the way knowledge was written and talked about: the prevailing emphasis of the Enlightenment on the rationalistic account of knowing had led to a disregard for any kind of "personal" knowing, and this, Polanyi believed, was a tragic misunderstanding of human experience. Belief, in the form of embodied commitment, is essential to knowing. Polanyi writes, "It is the act of commitment in its full structure that saves personal knowledge from being merely subjective. Intellectual commitment is a responsible decision, in submission to the compelling claims of what in good conscience I conceive to be true."[49]

Knowledge must be grounded in a subsidiary belief of one kind or another. In order to doubt proposition A you must believe in proposition B. You can doubt A precisely because you believe it is not B and so on. It is with this in mind that Polanyi sets out to make his knowledge claims. We may believe in order to know, and we may also make explicit statements in order to know. Tacit knowledge, however implicit and difficult to put into words, is experienced, acknowledged and established through practice. *We believe and do in order to know.*

Richard Gelwick suggests that the story of Archimedes and his discovery of the theory of displacement is an example of tacit knowing. He argues that Archimedes used his experience to guide

him to a major scientific discovery, but it happened unintention-
ally as a result of tacit knowledge. The body is an instrument that
we use in order to see and know the world; bodily subsidiary tacit
particulars guide and direct our observation and thinking. Archimedes' awareness of the problem and his subsidiary awareness of
the rise of water in the bathtub enabled him to find a coherent and
relevant meaning to these two sets of tacit particulars. Gelwick
writes:

> The structure of tacit knowing explains how we use our body to
> attend from it to things outside of it. When we rely upon clues,
> we interiorise and dwell in them as the proximal terms of our
> existence. That our knowing is always a form of indwelling is
> one of the revolutionary aspects of Polanyi's theory leading to a
> new paradigm. It overthrows centuries of dichotomies that have
> separated mind and body, reason and experience, subject and
> object, the knower and the known.[50]

Knowledge, for Polanyi, is often directly linked to practical
actions. Action breathes life into knowledge that we can only begin
to understand as we indwell it through action. As I stated earlier, the
magician is subsidiarily aware of the tacit details, but only insofar
as she relies on them in order to attend to the focal meaning of a
particular piece of sleight-of-hand magic. The magician embodies
the piece and performs it. Polanyi himself explains this:

> Our body is always in use as the basic instrument of our intel-
> lectual and practical control over our surroundings. Hence in all
> our waking hours we are subsidiarily aware of our body within
> our focal knowledge of our surroundings. And of course our
> body is more than a mere instrument.[51]

In other words, we are always acting in a bodily way as we focally attend to our everyday experience. We do not focus on the tacit particulars of walking, but we are aware of them and experience them bodily as we walk. We accept these tacit particulars and dwell in them as we dwell in our own bodies. Experience and practice are both embodied, and each informs and imposes on the other. Like the magician, I may intellectually know how to do the vanish, but until I have practised the sleight and embodied or indwelt the particulars, I will not be able to vanish the ball. Knowledge of the vanish is justified and acknowledged in an embodied way through the practice of the vanish. As Polanyi has stated, "This is why mathematical theory can be learned only by practising its application: its true knowledge lies in our ability to use it."[52] "True" knowledge for Polanyi is deeply rooted in practice.

Embodied practical actions rely on the tacit dimension. Tacit knowledge is required in order to practise as a doctor, magician, electrician or gastroenterologist. To do something is to know something, and to know something in a particular way. These unspecifiable particulars act as guideposts as we make our way through life doing a little of this and whole lot of that.

"The greatest enemy of knowledge is not ignorance it is the illusion of knowledge." —Stephen Hawking

THE ART OF DOING

Ian Hacking, a prominent philosopher of science, suggests that we do in order to know.[53] Practical, hands-on experience is directly linked to making meaningful knowledge claims, and more importantly, is not just a detached claim about an experiment, but is one grounded in a practical knowledge of the experiment. Practice is indeed linked to the knowledge-making process. Moreover, practice is intervention, says Hacking: scientists practise as they intervene, and they intervene as they practise.

Similarly, Stephen Turner in his book *The Social Theory of Practice*s suggests that practice is connected to tradition, tacit knowledge, paradigms and presuppositions. Tradition must imply practice of one kind or another. Practices can be regarded as tacit habitual attitudes or as inarticulable competences or performances. Joseph Rouse, in his essay "Understanding Scientific Practices," corroborates this idea as he writes about the importance of scientific practice in experimental life. He argues that knowing is mediated socially by the knower, but also, more importantly, by the skills or practices that the knower employs. Rouse writes, "Knowing is mediated not only by a 'background' of beliefs but also by models, skills, instruments, standardized materials and phenomena and situated interaction among knowers, in short, by practices."[54] Rouse is clearly acknowledging the multi-layered aspect of knowledge.

These layers may appear, for example, in the simple exercises of writing, experimenting and, in short, living. As human beings, we are interacting with our world in an embodied and practical way. Experience presupposes (and produces) skilful engagement and cooperation with a host of unknown, worldly particulars. However simple or complex our experience may be, we must rely on and indwell skills of one form or another to live well.

Rouse is particularly interested in the role that these embodied practices play in the life of the scientist, and how they in turn shape the relationship between the knower and the known. He contrasts a scientist's practical, hands-on understanding with a "knowledge" that consists of explicit rules or propositions. He also points out that the scientist is situated within a community and social ethos that will tacitly determine how she will conduct herself.

This echoes the claim that Steven Shapin has made with respect to experimental, practical life. How do the tacit particulars in experimental space and life alter or affect what the scientist will do, say and record? In his essay "The House of Experiment in Seventeenth-Century England," Shapin writes about the role of the public experimental space over and against the private experimental space. He suggests that knowledge requires and maintains a certain position with respect to the place of experiment, and argues that cultural standards and social settings and practices affected what was and was not regarded as knowledge in the seventeenth century. Particular spaces provide scientists with particular ways of behaving, and this tacit behaviour will affect how the scientist performs and practices within each specific setting. Shapin writes:

> In the middle of the seventeenth century the experimental laboratory and the places of experimental discourse did not have the

standard designations, nor did people who found themselves within them have any tacit knowledge of the behavioral norms obtained there.[55]

Tacit knowledge was required in order to behave in the customary way in the laboratory. Shapin also recognizes that the laboratory came with a social context and that there were "rules" or "norms" associated with these spaces that imposed upon experimental life and in turn determined how scientists behaved in the laboratory. He describes some of the practices that governed the making and recognition of statements of "fact"; such statements were never disinterested and were not made without some kind of prior tacit consent on the part of the scientific community as part of the wider society. Social convention played a specific role in the formulation of knowledge, but more importantly it formed a part of the tacit dimension that imposed itself on the life of the seventeenth-century scientist.

PRACTICE MAKES PERFECT

In a similar way to that of Shapin's more comprehensive approach Hacking too argues that the grounds for scientific belief involve much more than merely making observations about phenomena and matching them to theoretical hypotheses. Justified belief involves "hands-on" reasoning as well. What makes an experiment convincing, he says, is the scientist's ability to get a complex trial working well enough that she knows the data it is going to provide will have some significance. This "hands-on" approach is rooted in practice and relies heavily on the tacit dimension. He writes, "The final arbitrator in philosophy is not how we think but what we do."[56] For Polanyi, too, any skill is as much an art of doing as it is an art of knowing.[57] Specific practical action, insists Hacking, is a prerequisite for effective, practical knowing. Knowledge is not merely something that can be drawn from a textbook or laboratory; knowledge is not only theoretical. He reminds us that philosophers of science have "gone overboard for theory at the expense of the experiment."[58]

Even observation, says Hacking, is a skill in that it is not directly linked to theory. It is not merely stating or reporting; observation in the sense of recording data is only one aspect of experimental science. In observing, one relies on a tacit knowledge, developed through experience, of what to look for and what is relevant or significant. If observation is a skill and it does lead to knowledge, as Hacking maintains, then why does this integral and important aspect of scientific experimentation not make it into finished reports of a specific experiment? He suggests that the history and philosophy of science has traditionally ignored the implications of the skill involved in observation. He writes, "A philosophy of experimental science cannot allow theory-dominated philosophy to make the very concept of observation become suspect."[59] It is this type of theory-dominated suspicion that drove Polanyi to pursue philosophy. His notion of the tacit dimension is rooted in practice, tradition and a commitment to a knowing community. The heavy emphasis on theory did not allow the many nuances associated with the practice of science to emerge. Polanyi's goal was to redirect some of that theory-centric focus.

Jerry Gill echoes this notion of theoretical prominence in his book *The Tacit Mode*:

> Polanyi believed that throughout history Western philosophy has defined knowledge far too narrowly, thereby overlooking

both its deep nature and its broader significance; it has almost completely ignored the tacit dimension or mode of all epistemological endeavour.[60]

Polanyi and Hacking are both trying to present a more accurate understanding of how knowledge is acquired in experimental science. The dominance of theory over practice has changed how science is practised. Hacking writes, "The harm comes from a single-minded obsession and thinking about theory, at the expense of intervention and action and experiment."[61] He is looking for a new understanding of the relationship between history, experiment and observation, a more comprehensive account of scientific life that includes the practical and hands-on aspect of all experimentation. "Philosophers of science constantly discuss theories and representations of reality," he writes, "but say almost nothing about experiment, technology, or the use of knowledge to alter the world."[62]

Polanyi would agree. He suggests that a scientist's participation or personal knowledge is what will and ultimately must direct the skills that a scientist will use. This personal knowledge is grounded in the tacit dimension. Polanyi writes, "Science is operated by the skill of the scientist and it is through the exercise of his skill that he shapes his scientific knowledge."[63] The experience of practice itself directs the scientist. Tacit particulars rise to the surface and can be attended to focally only in and through practice.

> Indeed, the premises of a skill cannot be discovered focally prior to its performance, nor even understood if explicitly stated by others, before we ourselves have experienced its performance, whether by watching it or by engaging in it ourselves.[64]

Science is in experimenting, practising and doing, but according to Hacking, the history of the natural sciences nowadays is almost always written as a history of theory. Francis Bacon taught that we must observe nature as it presents itself to us, or, as Hacking writes, "in the raw," and that we must manipulate this world in order to learn its secrets and the knowledge that lies hidden behind its natural order. It's interesting to note that when the Royal Society of London was founded in 1660, demonstration in science became popular and even essential; Hacking asserts that the Society was interested in theory but always included the role of observations, experiments and the resulting deductions. Robert Hooke and Robert Boyle, for example, two important practising scientists of the day, would never have addressed the Royal Society without some kind of demonstration. Intervention played an important role in science and how it was recorded. But times have changed, says Hacking. "History of the natural sciences is now almost always written as a history of theory. Philosophy of science has so much become philosophy of theory that the very existence of pre-theoretical observations or experiments has been denied."[65]

Practice is critical and involves a type of knowledge that can only be transmitted through example. In order for a doctor to be effective, she must be able to recognize certain symptoms so as to make a relevant diagnosis. Polanyi maintains that there is no point in simply reading a description of symptoms; understanding here is only meaningful in the context of a demonstration that gives rise to practical, hands-on knowledge. The same is true of any complex task of recognition and classification. "Although the expert diagnostician, taxonomist and cotton-classer can indicate their clues and formulate their maxims, they know many more things than they can tell, knowing them only in practice, as instrumental particulars, and not explicitly, as objects."[66] Moreover, this demonstration, Polanyi suggests, must occur within an apprentice-like tradition. The relationship of master and apprentice is essential for transmission of this kind of knowledge. It is within this relationship that inarticulate particulars will be communicated.

Recognition, then, or the diagnostician and others, depends on tacit knowing. Polanyi clarifies this with an example of a medical student who first learns a textbook list of bones, arteries and nerves. A certain kind of knowledge is gained by this means, but it is of little value, because until the student has seen these organs in relationship to the other organs that surround them, a clear understanding of anatomy can never develop. It is through the technique of dissection and surgery that a meaningful and relevant knowledge of anatomy will grow. The subsidiary awareness of the relationship of one organ to another that arises from this hands-on activity will affect how a doctor will focally attend to the situation at hand and arrive at a diagnosis. The skill of anatomical recognition depends on practical intervention:

> [T]he characteristics of the body can usually be clearly identified by diagrams. The major difficulty in the understanding, and hence in the teaching of anatomy, arises in respect to the intricate three-dimensional network of organs closely packed inside the body, of which no diagram can give an adequate representation.[67]

This three-dimensionality is of particular interest, because it points to the importance of hands-on interaction with the real thing in the real world. This is not to say that there is no meaningful knowledge to be acquired through a textbook; however, in a comprehensive account of how the doctor who practises medicine acquires his knowledge, one must include the link between theory and practice. Polanyi writes of textual accounts that "they are maxims, which can serve as a guide to an art only if they are integrated into the practical knowledge of the art. They cannot replace this knowledge."[68]

Ian Hacking uses the example of looking through a microscope to illustrate his claim that doing through intervention is a pathway towards knowledge. He regards the pre-theoretical role of what he calls "fiddling around" as important and necessary for the advancement of microscopy. This "fiddling around" is a form of practice. He finds that philosophers generally tend to see microscopes as black boxes that use a light source to view things at one end from a hole made to look through on the other. "[Y]ou learn to see through a microscope by doing, not just looking,"[69] he writes, suggesting that without some reference points, comparative analysis or experience of using and acting with and around microscopes, the untrained user may see through the lens, but will not necessarily know what it is they are seeing. Meaningful sight is acquired through meaningful practical intervention; without a tacit reference point established in this way, the image is simply a meaningless, magnified blob. Hacking writes, "Practice – and I mean in general doing, not looking – creates the ability to distinguish between visible artifacts of the preparation or the instrument, and the real structure that is seen with the microscope."[70] Again we see a connection between practice, the tacit dimension and meaningful knowledge.

We can also see this in the use of language. Use a word without a tacit coefficient or reference point, and it is utterly meaningless.

Words must be used contextually if we are to know what they mean. If, for example, in the middle of a conversation, a word is uttered that we do not recognize or "see" as belonging in the context, we will not understand how and why the word has been used, nor what it means. It is only through the practice of using the word that we understand the word and how it relates to the sentence and the conversation. Consider the decontextualized encounter with a new word, such as *pectinate*. Without a reference point, the word is for all intents and purposes meaningless, even if I know the dictionary definition. Until I have put it into practice or observed others doing so, my apprehension of it will be elementary at best. *Pectinate*, according to the dictionary, has something to do with tooth-like projections; having read this definition, I apprehend something about the word, but it seems to me that I have not assimilated its true meaning. A richer and fuller comprehension will come only though practice. This is a good example of Polanyi's notion of indwelling. We come to know words not by memorizing their meaning from a textbook, but by experiencing their use (and misuse) in context. Words are indeed like tools: I may know what a tool (such as a microscope) is used for, but if I do not have practical knowledge of how to use it, it is useless to me. Language, like the microscope, must be grounded in practice to make meaningful contact with reality.

In a lecture to the Royal Society, Polanyi tells a humorous and revealing story about an object he brought home with him from a visit to the United States.[71] It was an instrument of some kind. He did not know exactly what it was or what it was used for; it was only after he returned to the States that he found out what its purpose was. It was designed to puncture two holes in a beer can simultaneously. No scientific analysis could have told Polanyi this, even though he might have observed, from examining its physical structure, that there were two points or cutting surfaces on the instrument. However, someone who had used the instrument in daily practice could not only describe for him directly what it was for and how it was used, but could demonstrate its use for him. Knowledge and practice are linked.

Practice, or intervention (they amount to the same thing), not only contributes to, but is essential to, the production of what counts as scientific knowledge. There is no demonstrable reason to value theory over practice. The "art of doing," as Polanyi would call it, is very much a part of the experimental process and must be valued as such. He writes, "[P]ractical wisdom is more truly embodied in action than expressed in rules of action."[72] And as we have seen, without the tacit component of this art of practical intervention, one cannot *do* in an appropriate and meaningful way.

THE ART OF OBSERVATION

In Representing and Intervening, Hacking discusses the nature of observation and its primary role in the acquisition of knowledge. According to Hacking, however, observations and the statements they encourage are skill-oriented: that is, to observe and to make a statement based on observation is to exercise a skill developed through practice. He believes that too often "good science" is accounted for via a strict adherence to theory, while experiment and observation have assumed an inferior role not justified by the actual history of scientific discovery. He wants to reinterpret science according to a more practical model. Although he does not discuss the notion of tacit knowing at length, his emphasis on the skill involved in observation hints at it. He writes that some people are better at observation than others and that there is room for observational improvement through training and practice.[73]

> The good experimenter is often the observant one who sees the instructive quirks or unexpected outcomes of this or that bit of equipment. You will not get the apparatus working unless you are observant. Sometimes persistent attention to an oddity that would have been dismissed by a lesser experimenter is precisely what leads to new knowledge.[74]

Polanyi would argue that Hacking's references to "instructive quirks" and "persistent attention to oddities" and his notion of a "lesser experimenter" are all indications of practical, hands-on, tacit knowledge. Sometimes an observer acts in a way that is not formally recognizable. She may notice and pursue things that less experienced observers do not. The quirks and oddities that arrest her attention are part of the subsidiary particulars on which she has come to rely. It is only through the practice of experimentation that quirks and oddities of this kind can be practically noticed and incorporated into reliable, experimental accounts.

Hacking even speaks of the "gifted" observer. He argues that sometimes it is precisely a *lack* of explicit theory, a lack that results in the free play of one's skill and experience, that enables one to see things others may not readily observe. Traditional philosophers of science suggest that theory must precede any relevant and meaningful observations, but Hacking disagrees: observations are not necessarily grounded in theory, but in practical, hands-on experience. He gives the example of the lab assistant who, lacking any specific theory, is enabled by extensive practice in reading photographic plates to notice positron tracks appearing on one of them. By indwelling the practice, the observer is able to generate meaningful claims:

> An assistant can be trained to recognize those tracks without having a clue about theory. In England it is still not too uncommon to find a youngish lab technician, with no formal education past 16 or 17, who is not only extraordinarily skilful with the apparatus, but also quickest at noting an oddity on for example the photographic plates he has prepared from the electron microscope.[75]

Caroline Herschel is another example. She discovered more comets than any other person in history: eight in a single year. Hacking notes the skills of her brother as an astronomer and implies that he had much to do with Caroline's abilities by acting as her mentor in that field. Her skill as an observer was developed through persistent, careful practice.[76] "Most important of all," writes Hacking, "she could recognize a comet at once."[77] She did not have knowledge of an explicit set of criteria involved in recognizing comets, yet she continued to discover them, not so much because of her exceptional visual acuity but because she was indwelling a tacit set of subsidiary particulars that enabled her to distinguish a comet from just another star. Her skill developed cumulatively as she engaged her experience, embodying the things she had been taught.

BOYLE, THE AIR-PUMP AND WHY HOBBES WAS WRONG

In their book *Leviathan and the Air-Pump*, Steven Shapin and Simon Schaffer argue that experimental replication is directly linked to basic-fact production in science.[78] They are interested in why experimental practices have counted as proper and dependable avenues to reliable knowledge. They suggest that the production of new knowledge of any kind must rest on a foundation of convention:

> Any institutionalized method for producing knowledge has its foundations in social conventions: conventions concerning how the knowledge is produced, about what may be questioned and what may not, about what is normally expected and what counts as an anomaly, about what is regarded as evidence and proof.[79]

Here again we can find the tacit dimension imposing on the life of the scientist, specifically with respect to issues surrounding the replicability of experiments. For, as they claim, "In replication, there is no unambiguous set of rules that allows the experimenter to copy the practice in question."[80] Shapin and Schaffer suggest that a transmission of skills is required if one is to replicate experiments, and that this comes about not merely by the physical reiteration of specific procedures, but through a "virtual witnessing" of the experiment itself. This knowledge, they insist, is rarely transmitted through diagrams and text.

Robert Boyle's research in pneumatics, particularly his construction of the air-pump, will serve to illustrate this point; Shapin and Schaffer note that this example from the history of science is an oft-told tale of how authentic scientific knowledge is secured, and they consider Boyle one of the most important contributors to our understanding of the value of experimental practice. They pay special attention to how, in the construction of the air-pump and its operation, facts were generated through social, technical and literary application, through a hands-on, practical approach in the form of a series of experiments. Personal transmission of skilful knowledge had immense significance for this process. Replicas of the air-pump were subsequently built, but "these machines have, to our knowledge, never been operational, and none of Boyle's air -pump experiments of the late 1650s and 1660s has been repeated in modern times."[81] Christiaan Huygens was the only scientist who was able to build one of Boyle's air-pumps without the hands-on direction of Robert Boyle and Robert Hooke.[82]

In other words, the presence of a "master" or a knowledgeable scientist was a crucial requirement for the successful transmission of specific skills; the primary conditions for successful air-pump construction were obtained only when the "master" was present. Shapin and Schaffer write, "No one built a version of Boyle's machine without such experience. No one relied on Boyle's textual description alone."[83] Huygens, who was present at the air-pump trials in London in the spring of 1661, and who then built his own pump in autumn of the same year, had experienced the personal transmission of craft skill, picking up the necessary particulars in person and through practical demonstration. Polanyi argues that this is precisely the type of situation in which the artful skill of doing must be transmitted in person, passed on from master to apprentice; it is an "elbow knowledge" of sorts. Diagrams and text were helpful, but the tacit subsidiaries could not be transmitted through the written description alone, nor simply by verbal instruction. An inarticulate set of skills had to be relied on in order to hand this knowledge from one scientist to the other, and it is this that Polanyi refers to as tacit knowledge.

These particulars are an essential part of all practical skill, and their personal transmission involves trust and submission to authority, as Polanyi indicates:

To learn by example is to submit to authority. You follow your master because you trust his manner of doing things even when you cannot analyze and account in detail for its effectiveness. By watching the master and emulating his efforts in the presence of his example, the apprentice unconsciously picks up the rules of the art, including those which are not explicitly known to the master himself. These hidden rules can be assimilated only by a person who surrenders himself to that extent uncritically to the imitation of another. A society which wants to preserve a fund of personal knowledge must submit to tradition.[84]

Boyle, Hooke and Huygens were involved in this type of personal contact. Their learning environment was grounded in relationships of trust, and those relationships were established and expressed in personal, practical action. They worked closely together, and the results of their science were determined largely through the master-apprentice relationship.

Huygens had access to a set of skills that he had difficulty describing and articulating textually. As a teacher, he had to rely on his practical ability and the inarticulable dimension of his personal instruction. To guarantee the performance of the pumps, Huygens, Hooke or Boyle had to be present at their construction. This turned out to be the case in several different sets of air-pump trials in London, France and Holland. When these individuals were present, the transmission of their craft and skill was effective. Shapin and Schaffer write, "Thus, if replication is the technology which turns belief into knowledge, then knowledge production depends not just on the abstract exchange of paper and ideas but on the practical social regulation of men and machines."[33]

This notion of "social regulation" involved the development, especially by people in positions of influence, money and prestige, of a set of practices adhered to by people engaged in experimental work. This unwritten set of rules was a large part of Hobbes' point about the social construction of knowledge in the laboratory; as Shapin and Schaffer have noted, "Knowledge, as much as the state, is the product of human actions. Hobbes was right."[86] Social order, privilege and position imposed on the way knowledge was constructed. The quality, content and sources of justification were often subordinated to questions that were more concerned with who and where than what and how. Yet Hobbes was also wrong: the construction of knowledge is not *merely* a social concern. Knowledge is not just a by-product of social convention. This type of reductionism is exactly what Polanyi was reacting against. He believed in a fuller and more comprehensive account of knowledge as a whole.

THE PERSONAL AND THE SUBJECTIVE

Upon a first reading of *Personal Knowledge* one could, if not reading carefully, be led to believe that Polanyi was a subjectivist. The title alone might give rise to such a misunderstanding. However, Polanyi was not a subjectivist; he did believe in a reality that could ultimately be known. Subjectivity is not the same as subjectivism.

The confusion arises from the fact that, as Jerry Gill has suggested, "The term objectivity has become the password for knowledge in the modern era."[87] By "objectivity" we are referring to a type of knowing that is traditionally exalted, among philosophers of science, as impersonal, detached and always explicit. The history of science clearly shows that a rejection of all things personal was a central part of the scientific or Enlightenment project: every effort was made to eliminate personal knowledge from science and philosophy. How is this possible? Every judgement call of a philosopher or scientist must be intensely personal. As Harry Prosch has observed, "Personal judgment must always decide what weight to attach to any particular set of evidence."[88]

The whole of Polanyi's project is to be understood as an attempt to counteract the one-sided emphasis on objectivity.[89] Polanyi argues that all rational activity must operate between two poles of understanding: the subjective and the objective. The subjective is the knowing, acting, believing person; the objective is the other, a community or reality independent of the knower herself. Personal knowledge is about the knower interacting with reality as she looks away from herself. Polanyi illustrates this with the example of a blind man using a stick to explore a cavern.[90] The blind man is tacitly aware of the stick and does not notice it explicitly; he is focally aware of the reality of the cave presently at hand, and he submits to it, making meaningful contact with it. This is the objective reality situated within the tacit, personal knowledge of the knowing subject. Polanyi writes of personal experience that "we live in it as in the garment of our own skin."[91] It is a knowledge that is objectively grounded and yet intensely personal. In other words, claims to objectivity can *only* be made from within a personal and human dimension. Any attempt to ignore this personal dimension is absurd. Objective knowledge claims can never be objective in the sense of being divorced from human experience, whether philosophical, religious or scientific. Prosch writes that Polanyi had "almost from the beginning, as we have seen, recognized the absurdity of this attachment to detachment."[92]

It is important to remember that Polanyi was not arguing that personal knowledge necessarily leads to the establishment of truth; that would indeed be subjectivism. As Jerry Gill writes, "Rather, he is claiming that without this personal aspect the whole epistemological enterprise makes no sense because it constitutes the *raison d'être* for seeking knowledge in the first place."[93] Polanyi was trying to establish a new and more comprehensive approach, an alternative to mere subjectivism on the one hand and detached objectivism on the other. He saw both of these polar positions as forms of reductionism, and was interested in something more than an either/or distinction. He writes,

> In so far as the personal submits to requirements acknowledged by itself as independent of itself, it is not subjective; but in so far as it is an action guided by individual passions, it is not objective either. It transcends the disjunction between subjective and objective.[94]

In other words, personal knowledge is not something founded on mere emotional whimsy; one does not make a knowledge claim based on private feelings or impressions. "That there are no exact rules for acquiring knowledge, however, does not mean that the whole matter is arbitrary or subjective; far from it,"[95] writes Marjorie Grene. Arbitrary claims are avoided by indwelling a particular community of knowers and submitting to the compelling claims of reality. Personal knowledge claims must indeed appeal to the nature of the evidence in question, but evidence is apprehended through adherence to a set of skills, tacit knowledge, tradition and authority, all of which represent the notion of the "personal" engaging with the world in practical, embodied ways.

The act of knowing and knowledge itself will always be situated within an embodied and personal knower. This is the subject; hence Polanyi's insistence on the subjectivity of knowing. By including scientific knowing within this personal domain, he was attempting to rehumanize it and abolish the illusion of distance between the knower and the known. As Richard Gelwick writes, "The scientific outlook imbued with the objective ideal has led to an absurd view of the universe because it has tried to know without having a place for the risks and the faith of the knower who is at the centre of this inquiry."[96] To know is to invest; it is to act. We act and we invest in a personal manner, rooted in bodily human experience. This is what makes knowledge human and personal. However, personal knowledge is not "personal" in the sense of private, independent or individualistic, confined to the individual's head, because it is also rooted in tradition and authority. Tradition; authority; the practical relation between subsidiary and focal aspects of tacit knowledge; practice and the art of doing; commitment to truth; submission to an overarching reality: these are all clues that help us distinguish Polanyi's notion of "personal knowledge" from subjectivism. He writes,

> Such is the *personal participation* of the knower in all acts of understanding. But this does not make our understanding subjective. Comprehension is neither an arbitrary act nor a passive experience, but a responsible act claiming universal validity. Such knowing is indeed *objective* in the sense of establishing contact with a hidden reality...[97]

As I have said earlier, commitment is essential to this kind of knowing. By committing to the compelling claims and authority of a tradition that one indwells, and by submitting to a community of knowers and to a reality beyond that community, one can and one does make "personal" knowledge claims. "It is the act of commitment in its full structure," writes Polanyi, "that saves personal knowledge from being merely subjective. Intellectual commitment is a responsible decision, in submission to the compelling claims of what in good conscience I conceive to be true."[98] Every act of judgment by the scientist and philosopher alike is indeed intensely "personal"; elsewhere Polanyi writes:

> Consider the fact that each scientist follows his own personal judgment for believing any particular claim of science and each is responsible for finding a problem and pursuing it in his own way; and that each again verifies and propounds his own results according to his personal judgment.[99]

These judgments are always situated in a human context and are entirely personal acts. Marjorie Grene writes, "Polanyian personal knowledge, rooted in society and demanding active submission to a tradition, even if sometimes in partial rebellion against it, is nevertheless knowledge: a claim to be in touch with a reality beyond and independent of the claimant."[100]

As discussed earlier, knowledge is transmitted from master to apprentice, is rooted in personal commitment and is communicated with a community of people who do, who practise, who know and who invest. It is this knowing community that Polanyi points and appeals to. The scientist must act on her own judgment and commit, but must also submit to the authority of the tradition within which she practices. Richard Gelwick writes, "Knowledge, whether in the routine application of previous achievements or in the creative discovery of new frontiers, is always an act of human responsibility."[101] Scientists are responsible to a community beyond themselves. There are common notions of value, standards and consensus that the scientist must submit and appeal to even when committing to a view that differs from the established one. The collective body of knowledge acts as a guide and filter, sifting out the private and subjective whims of individuals and calling them to consider the larger context of the shared scientific project. Responsibility and trust are therefore essential. Jerry Gill writes, "Unless we trust our powers of perception, scientific knowledge is clearly out of the question; likewise with our powers to make reasonable judgments in general."[102]

Tradition and authority can, of course, sift out too much, especially when ideas first emerge; that is the risk one takes when accepting one's responsibility to a community. Mendel was a nineteenth-century Austrian plant breeder who found that his early genetic research on pea plants supported the evolutionary particle theory of inheritance. He was accused by the originator of the theory, Carl Nageli, of presenting results that were too empirical or practical rather than rational. It wasn't until much later, when the notion of evolution was generally accepted and its force established, that Mendel's ideas were acknowledged to be correct. Mendel's personal judgment was right; his commitment and his "personal knowledge," arising from his observational skills, his practice and his submission to the compelling claims of objective reality, were directing him in a truthful manner. He committed to his theory long before the great body of evidence confirmed that his thinking was on solid ground. However, the particularly authoritarian stance of the scientific community in which he worked did not allow for his revolutionary biological account. At first his results were not noticed or accepted, and his observations were regarded as merely subjective and too practical. Mendel was wrong according to the tradition, but today we know otherwise.

Responsibility to a community beyond oneself rescues Polanyi's notion from the subjectivist critique, but it does so at the cost of occasionally delaying the recognition of knowledge. The scientific or philosophical community will help to "police" individual and subjective flights of epistemic fancy. Again, judgments are personal, but not private; they are rooted in tradition and committed to a more fundamental whole that is shared by the community. History has shown that sometimes the community may be wrong; however, this is how communities operate. Both the individual and the community must trust that ultimately the compelling claims of reality will make themselves known as knowers interact with the world in an embodied way.

Science and philosophy must work from within an accepted set of rules, formulae and presuppositions. It is from within this structure that one can move, operate and make philosophical and scientific claims. Jerry Gill, discussing responsibility with regard to these claims, writes, "[C]onclusions need to be hammered out in the give and take of responsible dialogue among those who know and care about the field of inquiry involved and under the sanctions imposed by our mutual commitment..."[103]

Philosophy and science can never be pursued in a detached way, and can never be a matter of pure conceptual articulation. Scientists indwell and adhere to a particular community, and their knowledge will be social, historical and interpersonal. It will also be skilful, embodied, active and entirely human.

"I was gratified to be able to answer promptly, and I did. I said I didn't know." —Mark Twain

Albert Einstein wrote of a finite but unbounded universe. I will take his notion and expand on it ever so slightly and suggest the idea of an open-structured approach to knowledge that is grounded in what I have called epistemic humility.[104] That sounds wordy, but simply put it is an embodied approach, rooted in a rational recognition of the tacit dimension – the little things that are part of all our knowledge claims and experience – and the role it plays in our lives. It affects the way we see, live and interpret our experience. Acknowledged in such a way, the tacit dimension can act as a guidepost or pathway to how and what we know, establishing an open structure in which one can begin to speak of truth and knowledge from within other traditions that typically have not been acknowledged by the philosopher and the scientist. In this universe the liberal arts, poetry and other inarticulable ways of being can and often do produce knowledge. Other avenues to truth then give us a broad path to travel as opposed to a narrow one restricted by prejudiced understanding. Epistemic humility is a willingness to seriously entertain the Other's point of view; it is a tacit acceptance of the fact that we may be wrong about something.

A rational approach exercised with humility can open doors and eyes. When I claim to know this or that, what about the possibility of my being wrong? Polanyi writes about the nature of this possibility:

The construction of a framework which will handle experience on our behalf begins in the infant and culminates in the scientist. This endeavour must occasionally operate by demolishing a hitherto accepted structure, or parts of it, in order to establish an even more rigorous and comprehensive one in its place.[105]

This, I believe, is how most science and philosophy is practised. However, if the critique of the Cartesian worldview is still applicable, how far down does this potential for the recognition of error go? Epistemic humility opens one up to the potential for more comprehensive and meaningful dialogue. Consider two people in the middle of an argument. One says A, but the other has no desire to hear A and is only interested in presenting B. This is the antithesis of epistemic humility. These two interlocutors may feel as if they are involved in a dialogue when in fact one of them is intent only on presenting his own position. In such a "conversation" there is no openness or intimacy, in the sense of two people being vulnerable enough to genuinely encounter one another; there is neither relational contact nor connection. A better posture would be to commit to position A, as Polanyi would suggest, while remaining genuinely wide open to the possibility of B. Dialogue, it seems to me, recognizes the Other and the potential legitimacy of the Other's position, and it leads to dynamic growth. When we are dwelling in a state of openness and epistemic humility, we will be prepared to consider "demolishing a hitherto accepted structure."

When we are committed to open-structured thinking and epistemic humility, we acknowledge the possibility that we may be wrong; however, I believe we can simultaneously acknowledge the positive and creative aspects of the personal epistemological project. We may rely on a structure to guide our observation and thinking, but we are never constrained by it. We are committed to a structure, but it is not a closed structure; we remain open to guidance and often correction by the Other, through practice, a shared community of tradition and the compelling claims of reality. Operating from an open structure and within an ethos of humility, we recognize implicitly and dynamically that we may be wrong, but we also decide what we are going to do about it.

If tacit knowing is at the root of all knowing, as I have argued, then the greater part of our knowledge is hidden from our view; and if that is true, then I believe we are obliged to adopt an attitude of epistemic humility. Richard Gelwick uses the analogy of the iceberg to suggest this.[106] Most of the iceberg lies below the waterline, so that what we see is merely the tip of a much greater whole. If Polanyi is right, then it is the submerged part that alters how and what we know; what is hidden is, for the time being, not explicitly known. Typical accounts of knowledge are interested in and concerned with only the part that lies above. Gelwick writes,

> What we have been accustomed to call knowledge is like the peak of an iceberg, and we have neglected the greater part of knowledge itself because it is hidden from our direct view when we are using it.[107]

As we indwell a certain set of subsidiary particulars, we are able to focus on what lies before us. What if our subsidiaries are misguided, improperly informed, outdated? Polanyi writes, "When we accept a certain set of pre-suppositions and we use them as our interpretative framework, we may be said to dwell in them as we do in our own body."[108] His comment about embodiment is clear; just as we feel at home in our body and take it for granted, not focusing on it as we do things in it, so it is with our subsidiary particulars and our presuppositions. We may be unaware that we are working from a deficient set of subsidiary particulars. But if we operate in a spirit of epistemic humility, then our embodied experience and our encounter with other perspectives will reveal our presuppositions for what they are. Ernest Hemingway said that "[w]e are all apprentices in a craft where no one ever becomes a master." We live in a world of wonders that does not always fit into explicit definitions. This is what philosophy and life are all about: not restricting our thinking, but opening up what might lie ahead, the unknown and the not-yet.

There is no personal knowing without risk. If, as I showed earlier, we acknowledge the tacit effect of particulars, our levels of commitment, the influence of our social context and so on, we should be able to see the limitations of what and how we know. Polanyi echoes this sentiment on the last few pages of *Personal Knowledge*, describing the epistemological enterprise as that which "comprises everything in which we may be totally mistaken."[109] So, while we know more than we can tell, we must be careful not to tell more than we know. We must be open to being wrong and regard all knowledge claims as approximations and works in progress.

WORKING FREELY WITHIN STRUCTURES

A "finite and yet unbounded universe"[7] is a bit like a circle. The circular line has no beginning and no end; it has a finite size but no endpoints. The universe is limited in size, but ever expanding. The geometry is similar to that of the surface of a sphere or globe: if I began walking on a sphere I could continue walking forever. The surface and size of the sphere is finite, but there is no limit to the distance that I might travel.

It is the notion of the "yet" that interests me most in Einstein's description. The "yet" implies the potential for future discovery and change. I may know this or that, and yet...there may be something else I do not know which will impinge on my claim. "Yet" is an affirmation of the approximate nature of all knowledge claims; it implies that there is something more. We live in a structure that is open and adjustable. Reality may be real and it may be knowable, but we are always limited in our understanding of it and therefore must be open to the possibility of the "yet" which is "not yet" – not yet experienced. That is epistemic humility.

Our understanding and interpretation of reality is bound by our own limited structures, and yet I believe that we can operate freely within those structures. Einstein argues, with what he calls a "moderate degree of certainty," that notions of closed spaces without limits are conceivable; he believes the general theory of relativity allows for this.[110] The acceptance of a "moderate degree of certainty" indicates an open-structured universe and a willingness to assume risk: the risk of error, and the risk of having to change one's paradigm. As Marjorie Grene has written, "But in the search for knowledge, it is nevertheless truth, not subjectivity, that we are after, and if we may be wrong, we may also be right, although we can never know for certain that we are so."[111] We do, for the most part, favour closed systems; they are more comfortable and easier to understand. They depend on a denial of personal risk. On the other hand, open-structured thinking and epistemic humility may prevent lost opportunity, for they are concerned with a richer and more comprehensive opening up of the mind. It is a readiness to break out of accepted structures that may be wrong and hold us back. As we saw earlier on, Carl Nageli thought that Mendel's science was too empirical. His lack of open-structured thinking did not allow him to see the possibilities in Mendel's practically rooted account. He denied the notion of the "yet" that is "not yet."

Consider the creative opportunity found in a piano octave: twelve simple notes, but a vast musical landscape waiting to be discovered. This is open structure. There are sharps, flats, major chords and minor chords, harmonies and dissonances, this scale and that scale. There is an array of starting points and intervals giving rise to an infinity of tonal sequences that constitute melodies. The pianist travels through the scale, returns and resolves. Musical tension is created. There are any number of tempos – adagio, allegro, largo – and any number of rhythms, combined in different ways. There are texture and dynamics, crescendo, decrescendo, pianissimo, dolce, con brio, cantabile. The structure is restricted by a finite number of keys, but is open and presents limitless possibilities.

Drusilla Scott writes, "If we believe that nothing is reliable knowledge unless it is clear and explicit and testable by experiment, then we cannot know anything about intangible things like justice, love, purity, compassion or beauty."[112] With a spirit of epistemic humility at the forefront, it seems to me that we will be open to others, other possibilities and other avenues to truth.

Let's return to where I began this whole discussion. As an electrician I have had years of practical, hands-on experience. I know a great deal about electricity and the nature of electrical work. I have some theory and plenty of practice. An engineer has plenty of theory and little, if any, practice. We electricians had a saying about engineers: "They may have designed it, but clearly they have never installed it." Blueprints represent theoretical aspects of the electrical world. However, when encountering a problem with respect to an engineer's design, the electrician almost always relies upon practice to see any project through to a satisfactory end. Blueprints only take one so far; often the blueprints we worked from were inadequate, lacking detail and in some cases unrealistic, if not impossible to follow. In our experience, it was practice and the tacit knowledge therein that brought about constructive resolution. Engineers did not install, hook up, troubleshoot or involve themselves in any practical, hands-on aspect of the trade; they lacked the practice and therefore the tacit knowledge that was required to arrive at a workable resolution. They only knew how to represent and draw a design based on explicit theory. Training in electrical theory combined with tacit knowledge arising from the practical, hands-on aspect of the trade exemplifies Cartesian explicitness on the one hand and Polanyian personal knowledge on the other. Together they shape the way electricians practise their trade.

It is important to note that Polanyi faced this question of personal knowledge from within the life of a practising scientist. He was attempting to go beyond explicit formulations; like the virtuous individual detailed in Aristotle's *Nicomachean Ethics*, Polanyi did not take "refuge in theory,"[113] but instead exercised his theory through his personal practice as a scientist. He became a scientist by doing science. Virtue, Aristotle claims, is acquired by doing just acts. It is this Aristotelian commitment to practice and doing that is echoed in Polanyi's claims and life.

Personal knowledge is grounded in the tacit dimension and anchored in subsidiaries established through practice, not theoretical certainties. Part of my goal has been to suggest that such knowledge, rooted in skill and personhood and informed by community and tradition, is indeed reliable and meaningful. It does make contact with reality. Coherent claims to knowledge, for Polanyi, had to be grounded in a personal commitment to truth; all knowing must begin here. He was searching for an authentic approach to knowledge that would take into account embodied human experience and interaction.

> For, as human beings, we must inevitably see the universe from a centre lying within ourselves and speak about it in terms of a human language shaped by the exigencies of human intercourse. Any attempt rigorously to eliminate our human perspective from our picture of the world must lead to absurdity.[114]

If we did not acknowledge the personal component of the tacit dimension, we would be ignoring elements of the real world that have serious implications for all philosophical, epistemological and scientific studies.

One element of a real-world, personal approach to knowledge is risk. The theory of Newtonian mechanics, regarded by many to be one of the greatest theories in the history of science, turned out to be wrong – or at least, right only up to a point. As Marjorie Grene has appropriately asked, does that mean we can abandon the claim to knowledge altogether?[115]

I think not. And that is a statement of the most personal kind.

TWENTY-TWO

GENTLE REMINDERS

"Every heart sings a song, incomplete, until another heart whispers back. Those who wish to sing always find a song. At the touch of a lover, everyone becomes a poet." —Plato

Poetry has never been my strong point. However, I do love to put pen to paper and try to express an emotion, describe a moment or just recollect in an interesting literary way. It's a tradition that I've followed for years.

I've included a few of what I think are some of my better pieces. In some regards the inclusion of a few of my poetic thoughts doesn't really connect with my overall project. Poetry, however, is about noticing the little things. It is about finding the meaningful in the sometime seemingly insignificant details that surround us and more often than not breathe life into us in ways we can't even begin to imagine. Real change is poetic as much as *Real Change is Incremental*.

Gretchen Sankey, a wonderful artist from Toronto, sketched several drawings in response to some of my poems from a few years ago. I appreciated her reflections and interpretations then as I still do now. It seems to me that her drawings have more to say than my often inadequate poetic expressions and gestures.

W.H. Auden said, "The table exists because I scrub it," in his Christmas Oratorio. A favourite line of mine. Not even sure what it means, but it still digs down deep into my soul. Some of the poems I enjoy the most are the hardest ones that I find to understand – Auden, Eliot, Yeats, Rumi, Ovid and others.

Words have a way of capturing moments, reflections and thoughts in a way that memories cannot. Put them together and you've created something even more lasting and worthwhile.

Poetry and love share a lot in common. Without them we would be lost, in a forest, on the street – locally and globally disconnected travelling here and there. And always trying to find our way back home.

"Hope" is the thing with feathers
That perches in the soul
And sings the tune without the words
And never stops at all,
And sweetest in the gale is heard;
And sore must be the storm
That could abash the little bird
That kept so many warm.
I've heard it in the chillest land
And on the strangest sea,
Yet never, in extremity,
It asked a crumb of me.

—Emily Dickinson

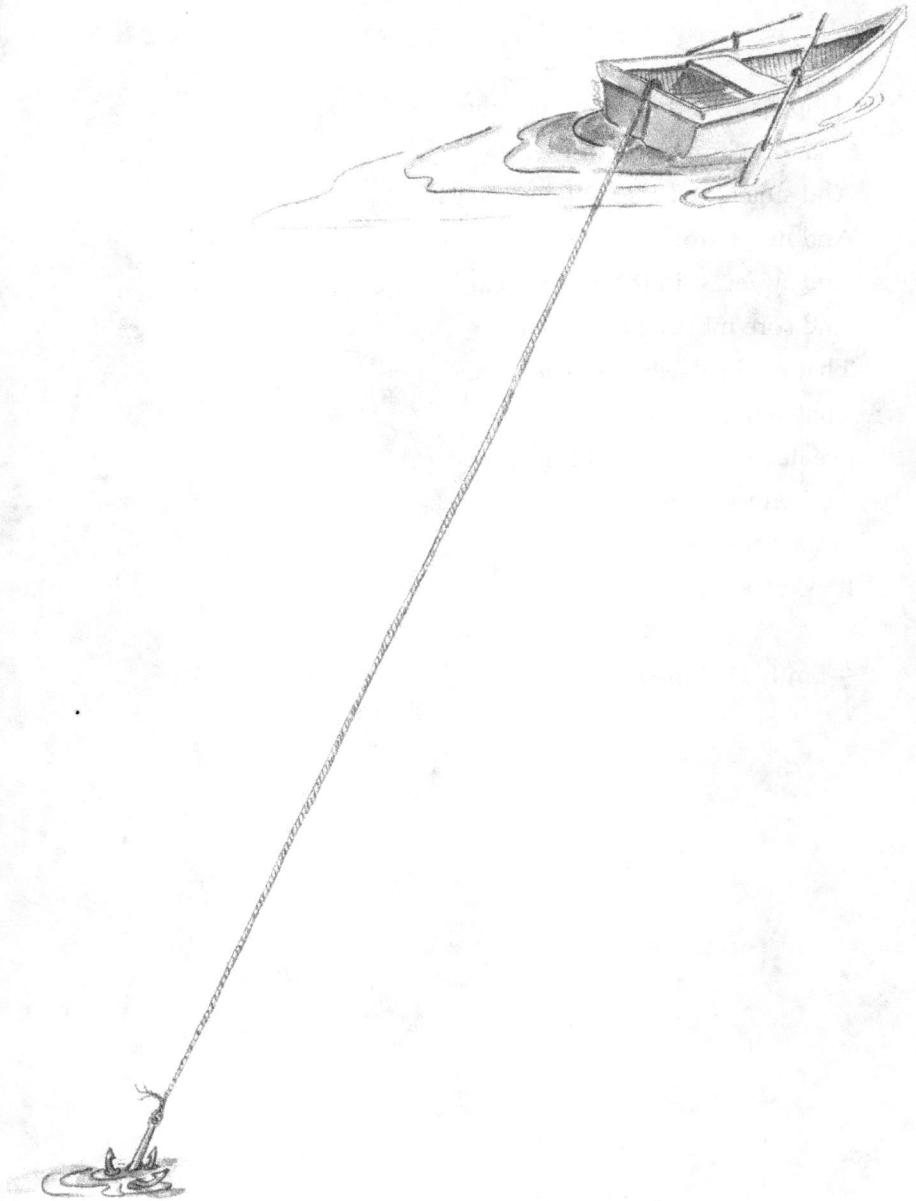

REAL CHANGE IS INCREMENTAL

STAYED AND STILL

gently
madly
merrily
rowing fro
rarely to.

motion-less
water
is stayed
still
around me.

dipping the oars
daring not
to rock
the boat
I continue dreaming.

REAL CHANGE IS INCREMENTAL

homeless
cold
forgotten

the skin
heart
and soul
longing
aching
demanding

the
tranquil security
found
within
the warmth
of
the human touch.

REAL CHANGE IS INCREMENTAL

UNDER THE BRIDGE

the water
under the bridge
is frozen.
the structure
balanced between
the cold and the spring thaw.

REAL CHANGE IS INCREMENTAL

what if...

$0>1$

$2+2 = 5$

$E=mc^3$

$a^2 + b^2 = c^3$

REAL CHANGE IS INCREMENTAL

SURROUNDED

on a good day the lint at the bottom of my pocket
barely reminds me of you.

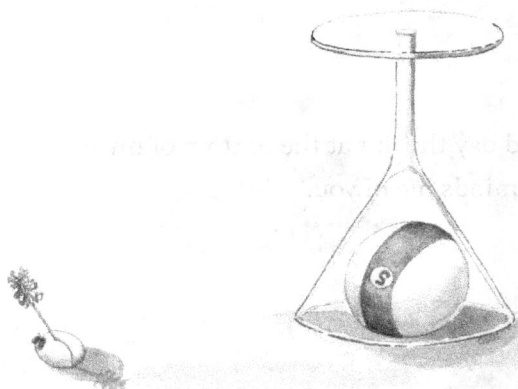

REAL CHANGE IS INCREMENTAL

on the break
between
you, me and the cue ball
our eyes met

martinis
card tricks,
edible lipstick

red-side pocket.

each glance
determined the trajectory
of my shot

chalking my cue
you smiled,
you laughed,
your presence,
enhanced the momentum
of the game.

yellow-side pocket.

each ball
glazed the green
and I wondered

the stripes,

the solids,
engaged in a precise conversation
and they moved,
and they touched,
and he trembled.

orange-side pocket

boston, eight ball, stripes and solids
tonight
i'll call it here and now.

from across the table top
hope
followed the game.

between
you, me and the cue ball.

i wondered

eight ball – corner pocket.

the uneasiness
and discouragement
unfolds like
firmly pressed
carefully pleated
wrapping paper
covering
the most cherished
of
Christmas gifts.

chosen, purchased and prepared
with the
utmost care
"Merry Christmas"
she says
as she
rips and tears
the fragile
covering away.

found later

balled up
and
unrecognizable.

resting amongst
embers

of hardwood trees
and
chestnut shells.
trapped.
between
hearth and chimney.
awaiting its
impending demise
in a blaze
of
flames, heat and light.

the remaining angry
gifts-wrapped
packaged
boxed up.

taped, ribboned.

looking oh so dull and gloomy.

an apprehensible exchange
on this
happy, joyous morning
celebrating
Christ's birth.

"Merry Christmas"
she says
"Merry Christmas"

"Merry Christmas"

and

"may your
     New Year
          be happy."

HEADFIRST

i've been standing
here for days now
unable to move
the children
kick, laugh and splash around me
they have no idea why they float
they just do

frozen
i'm still standing
knee deep
barely wet

bible in one hand
yardstick in the other
conducting some sort of
symmetrical
spiritual symphony
the notes drown
in the energy of the life around me

struggling with my lame attempt
at rational reconciliation
i watch as the book and the ruler
slip from my hands
they skim and wave their way through the water
resting one on top of the other
they form a cross at the bottom of the pool

smiling
i dive in headfirst into the drink
towards the shiny object

having just caught my eye
the light refracted off its metallic edge is my reminder
i trust it's a coin

a hopeful exchange
within the wishing well of life

the children's laughter
is muffled delight
as the water surrounds my ears
my eyes

open
covered
enveloped

tomorrow
i will drench the sun soaked couple sitting next to the edge of
this liquid blue sky

cannonballs are clear
crisp
and so much damn fun

CAPITAL

crack cocaine
and
coca-cola

street vendors approaching

you
and
your cash.

NOTES

FOUR STANDING ON THE EDGE

1   The following titles are references to some of the classical effects in magic considered to be among the greatest and simplest effects in the sleight-of-hand world. They consistently evoke emotional and surprised responses from most audiences as the effects are clear, simple and very difficult to reconstruct. They are considered classics for historical and in some cases nostalgic reasons.

    • Out of This World: Curry, Paul, *Magician's Magic* (Dover Publications, Mineola, NY, 2003).

    • Gypsy Thread: Buckingham, Geoffrey, *It's Easier Than You Think* (Magic Inc., Chicago, 1979).

    • Coin Matrix: Roth, David, *Expert Coin Magic* (D. Robbins & Co., Cranbury, NJ, 1985).

    • Triumph: Tannen, Louis, *Stars of Magic* (Louis Tannen Inc., New York, 1975).

SIX TO SEE

1   Dupré, Julie, *Skyscrapers* (Black Dog & Leventhal Publishers, New York, 2001), 114.

2   See <www.soulsystems.ca> for more information.

3   Wilson, Jonathan, *Vision That Grips You* (Leadership by Soul Newsletter, January 2011).

4   De Saint-Exupéry, Antoine, *The Little Prince* (Harvest Books, New York, 2001), 2.

SEVEN IN THE MOMENT

1   Descartes, René, tr. Voss, Stephen H., *The Passions of the Soul* (Hackett Publishing Company, Indianapolis, IN, 1989), 51–53.

2   Ibid., 56.

3   Fowles, John, "Seeing Nature Whole," *Harper's Magazine*, November 1979, 61.

4   Descartes, René, tr. Voss, Stephen H., *Discourse on Method* (Hackett Publishing, Indianapolis, IN, 1998), 3–5.

5   Ibid., 3–4.

6   Ibid., 3.

7   Ibid.

8   Ibid., 16.

9   Ibid., 18–50.

10   Ibid., 52.

11   Ibid., 61.

EIGHT RETIRED HUMANS

1   Sacks, Oliver, *The Man Who Mistook His Wife for a Hat* (HarperCollins, New York, 1970), 35–36.

2   For this chapter I will be referring to the version of *Blade Runner* known as the Director's Cut. This is the re-released film that removes the original voice-over and does not leave the viewer with a narrative "solution" at the end of the story. Questions arise throughout the film that remain unanswered. The Director's Cut does not seem concerned with directly addressing those specific questions and is more philosophical in tone than the original theatrical release.

3   To be authentic is to be human and fully aware of our past, present and future. It is to be conscious of our radical freedom and our ability to choose. Authenticity involves an understanding that we are in deep existential crisis as we have been thrown into a world not of our own making. See De Beauvoir, Simone, *The Ethics of Ambiguity* (Citadel Press, New York, 1976).

4   Bukatman, Scott, *Blade Runner* (London: British Film Institute, 1997), 67–86.

5   Baudrillard, Jean, *Simulations* (Semiotext(e), Columbia University, New

York, 1983), 57.

6   The self cannot even begin to discuss itself without an ability to interact with and remember the past. In short, the self is made and not a predetermined given. For further information see Jopling, David, *Self-Knowledge and the Self* (Routledge, New York, 2000).

7   A dystopia is a vision or critique of what will potentially be. Dystopias give us a collective indication of where humanity may be heading if we continue down certain political and socio-economic paths. *Blade Runner* exemplifies, and in some ways defines, the tradition behind the dystopic vision in science fiction films. "A combination of environmental destruction, late-capitalistic corruption, drug resistant diseases, and increasingly sophisticated electronic technology threatens human existence in 1990s science fiction. Human beings in science-fiction films have already lost their uniqueness to robots, androids, and cyborgs." Annette Kuhn, ed., *Alien Zone II* (Verso, New York, 1999), 203.

8   Ryan, Michael, and Kellner, Douglas, eds., *Camera Politica* (Indiana University Press, Indianapolis, IN, 1988), 255.

9   See Michel Foucault, *Discipline and Punish* (Vintage Books, New York, 1977) for a discussion of Panopticism. Foucault reminds us of the socialization of mind, body and soul via the confines of the architectural prison surrounding us – specifically in relation to prisons, the military, schools and hospitals. It seems to me that his thesis applies to the landscape and city of Los Angeles of 2019. The body and the self are implicitly refined, socialized and numbed through the city's social and environmental construction. It is not just architectural ingenuity at work, but an event in and of the human mind.

10   Wakefield, Neville, *Postmodernism: The Twilight of the Real* (Pluto Press, London, 1990), 118.

11   Clarke, David B., ed., *The Cinematic City* (Routledge, New York, 1997), 143–144.

12   In Sayer Karen, and Moore, John, *Science Fiction: Critical Frontiers* (St. Martin's Press, New York, 2000), 111.

13   Jean Baudrillard, op. cit., 4-5.

14   *Blade Runner*, Director's Cut, dir. Ridley Scott, Warner Brothers, 1982.

15   Annette Kuhn, ed., Alien Zone II (New York: Verso, 1999), 223.

16   Barthes, Roland, *Camera Lucida* (New York: Farrar, Straus & Giroux, 1981), 91.

17   Wakefield, Neville, op. cit., 117.

18   Ibid, 125.

19 An emotional assessment that the police use to determine emphatic responses from tested subjects. Deckard uses this to determine that Rachel is a replicant.

20 Bukatman, Scott, op. cit., 69.

TEN WHITE, WESTERN AND WAIST-DEEP

1 Hochschild, Adam, *King Leopold's Ghost* (Mariner Books New York, 1999), 15.

2 Anderson, Mary B., *Do No Harm* (Lynne Rienner Publishers, Boulder, CO, 1999).

3 Smillie, Ian, *Patronage or Partnership* (Kumarian Press, Boulder, CO, 2001), 176–177.

TWELVE EVERY BEAN YOU GRIND

1 <www.transfair.ca>.

2 Sachs, Jeffrey, *The End of Poverty* (Penguin Press, New York, 2005).

3 "The End of Poverty: An Interview with Jeffrey Sachs," by Onnesha Roychoudhuri, May 2005 <www.motherjones.com/news/qa/2005/05/ jeffrey_sachs.html>.

4 Aristotle, *Nicomachean Ethics*, in *Introduction to Aristotle*, McKeon, Richard, ed. (University of Chicago Press, Chicago, 1974).

5 <www.un.org/millenniumgoals>.

6 Talbot, John, *Grounds for Agreement* (Rowman & Littlefield, Oxford, 2004), 43.

7 Schumpeter, Joseph A., *The Process of Creative Destruction* (Edward Elgar Publishing, Chelthenham, UK, 1942).

8 Hochschild, Adam, *Bury the Chains* (New York: Mariner Books, 2006), 195.

FOURTEEN ARISTOTLE, MENTORSHIP AND ALEXANDER THE GREAT

1 *The Parables of Kierkegaard* (Princeton, NJ: Princeton University Press, 1989), 38.

FIFTEEN A CAUSAL DISCONNECT

1   According to CIDA, results-based management (RBM) is a program/project, life-cycle approach to management that integrates strategy, people, resources, processes and measurements to improve decision-making, transparency and accountability. The approach focuses on achieving outcomes, implementing performance measurement and learning and adapting, as well as reporting performance.

2   "The majority world" is a phrase I have adopted to refer to the Global South or those living in countries where the economic and the social gap is severe. The accepted terms for years have been the "third world" or "developing world"; for me they are problematic as they both assume far too much from our Western worldview.

3   See "Triple Bottom Line" in *The Economist*, November 17, 2009.

4   Avery, Christopher, "Cruelty Charges at Humane Society," *The Globe and Mail*, November 27, 2011.

5. Friedman, Milton, "The Social Responsibility of Business," *The New York Times Magazine*, September 13, 1970.

6   Lévinas, Emmanuel, *Totality and Infinity* (Duquesne University Press, Pittsburgh, PA, 1969), 187–197. See his writings for an ethical understanding of our relationship and responsibility to the Other through the "face-to-face" encounter.

7   Singer, Peter, "Famine, Affluence, and Morality," *Philosophy and Public Affairs 1*, no. 2 (spring 1972), 229–243.

SIXTEEN THE UNQUALIFIED POOR

1   Nutt, S., *Damned Nations* (Toronto: McClelland & Stewart, 2011), 153.

2   Singer, Peter, "Famine, Affluence, and Morality," *Philosophy and Public Affairs 1*, no. 2 (spring 1972), 229–243.

SEVENTEEN THE FACE, FORGIVENESS AND THE OTHER

1   Dallaire, R., *Shake Hands with the Devil* (Random House Canada, Toronto, 2003), 510–522.

2   See <www.sochange.ca> for more information.

3   Prison Fellowship International. See <www.pfi.org> for more information on their work in restorative justice.

4   Blake, William, "The Poison Tree," *Immortal Poems of the English Language* (Simon & Schuster, New York, 1952), 233.

5   Lévinas, Emmanuel, *Totality and Infinity* (Duquesne University, Pittsburgh, PA, 1969), 194–219.

6   Ibid., 213.

7   For further discussion on this "flight" from our freedom, see De Beauvoir, Simone, *The Ethics of Ambiguity* (Citadel Press, New York, 1976), 49–52.

8   Lévinas, Emmanuel, op. cit., 297.

9   Chan, Victor, *The Wisdom of Forgiveness* (Riverhead Books, New York, 2004), 117.

10 Ung, Loung, *First They Killed My Father: A Daughter of Cambodia Remembers* (HarperCollins, New York, 2000), 203–208.

11 Lévinas, Emmanuel, op. cit. (Duquesne University, Pittsburgh, PA, 1969), 46.

12 Critchley, S., and Bernasconi, eds., *The Cambridge Companion to Lévinas* (Cambridge UnIversity Press, New York, 2002), 6.

13 Lévinas, Emmanuel, op. cit., 247.

14 Ibid., 89.

15 Polanyi, Michael, *The Tacit Dimension* (Anchor Books, New York, 1967), 4–25.

16 Russon, J., *Human Experience: Philosophy, Neurosis, and the Elements of Everyday Life* (SUNY Press, New York, 2003), 33.

17 Dostoyevsky, F., *The Brothers Karamazov*, tr. Magarshack, D. (Penguin Books, London, 1958), 339.

18 Nietzsche, through the main character in *Thus Spoke Zarathustra*, prophesied that God was dead. As a philosopher he was suggesting that as a result of the failures in philosophy and religion God was now playing hide and seek. He was nowhere to be found. For Nietzsche this provided a rich ground for a new philosophy to be formulated that included a more comprehensive notion of what it means to be human

19 De Beauvoir, Simone, *The Ethics of Ambiguity* (Citadel Press, New York, 1976), 38–44.

20 Ibid., 35.

21 Ibid., 60–61.

22 Ibid., 73.

23 Lévinas, Emmanuel, op. cit. 218–219.

24 Tutu, Desmond, *No Future Without Forgiveness* (Image Books, New York, 2000), 31–32.

25 Niebuhr, R., *The Irony of American History* (University of Chicago Press, Chicago, 2008), 63.

26 Wilde, Oscar, "The Ballad of Reading Jail," *Collected Works of Oscar Wilde* (Wordsworth Editions Limited, Hertfordshire, UK, 1997), 747–765.

TWENTY-ONE PRACTICAL ACTION

1   Scott, Drusilla, *Everyman Revived* (Eerdmans Publishing, Grand Rapids, MI, 1995), 112.

2   OED definition.

3   Polanyi, Michael, *Personal Knowledge* (University of Chicago Press, Chicago, 1958), 49–65.

4   Polanyi, Michael, *The Tacit Dimension* (Anchor Books, New York, 1967), 4. Polanyi refers to how we may know a person's face. We can recognize it and yet we cannot usually tell how we recognize it. He will argue that we attend from subsidiary particulars while focally recognizing the face.

5   Grene, Marjorie, "Tacit Knowing: Grounds for a Revolution in Philosophy," *Journal of the British Society for Phenomenology 8*, no. 3, October 1977, 165.

6   Polanyi, Michael, *Personal Knowledge*, vii.

7   Gelwick, Richard, *The Way of Discovery* (Wipf and Stock Publishers, Eugene, OR, 2000), xvii.

8   Grene, Marjorie, op cit., 164. Grene speaks of Polanyi's work as being neglected by academic philosophers and "...ill appreciated even by many of those who have drawn heavily on his work."

9   Taylor, Charles, "Merleau-Ponty and the Epistemological Picture," *The Cambridge Companion to Merleau-Ponty*, Carman, Taylor, and Hansen, Mark B., eds. (Cambridge University Press, Cambridge, 2003), 27.

10 Gelwick, Richard, op cit., xvii.

11 Polanyi, Michael, *Personal Knowledge*, 203.

12 Plato, tr. West, Thomas G., and West, Grace Starry, *Texts on Socrates – The Apology* (Cornell University Press, New York, 1984), 69–72.

13 Ibid., 70–71.

14 Ibid., 71.

15 Rogers, Ben, "Pascal's Life and Times," *The Cambridge Companion to Pascal*, Hammond, Nicholas, ed. (Cambridge University Press, Cambridge, 2003), 8.

16 Polanyi, Michael, *The Tacit Dimension* (Anchor Books, New York, 1967), 22.

17 Ibid., 4.

18 Polanyi, Michael, *Personal Knowledge* (University of Chicago Press, Chicago, 1958), 49.

19 Polanyi, Michael, *The Tacit Dimension*, 10.

20 Scott, Drusilla, *Everyman Revived* (Eerdmans Publishing, Grand Rapids, MI, 1995), 10.

21 Polanyi, Michael, *Personal Knowledge*, 19.

22 Polanyi, Michael; Grene, Marjorie, ed., *Knowing and Being* (University of Chicago Press, Chicago, 1969), 144.

23 Gill, Jerry, *The Tacit Mode* (SUNY Press, New York, 2000), 57.

24 Khalfa, Jean, "Pascal's Theory of Knowledge," *The Cambridge Companion to Pascal*, Hammond, Nicholas, ed. (Cambridge University Press, Cambridge, 2003), 134.

25 Polanyi, Michael; Grene, Marjorie, ed., op. cit., 194.

26 Chomsky, Noam, *Aspects of the Theory of Syntax* (The MIT Press, Cambridge, MA, 1965), 58.

27 Polanyi, Michael; Grene, Marjorie, ed., op cit., 195.

28 Ibid.

29 Grene, Marjorie, "Tacit Knowing: Grounds for a Revolution in Philosophy," *Journal of the British Society for Phenomenology 8*, no. 3, October 1977, 165.

30 Polanyi, Michael, *Personal Knowledge*, 56.

31 Ryle, Gilbert, *Collected Papers, Volume Two* (Hutchinson, London, 1971), 218.

32 Stratton, G. M., "Vision Without Inversion of the Retinal Image," *Psychological Review 4*, 1897, 341–360 and 463–481.

33 Snyder, F. W. and Pronko, N. H., *Vision Without Spatial Inversion* (University of Wichita Press, Wichita, KS, 1952).

34 Polanyi, Michael; Grene, Marjorie, ed,, op cit., 198.

35 Ibid., 199–200.

36 Polanyi, Michael, *The Tacit Dimension*, 10.

37 Polanyi, Michael, *The Study of Man* (Routledge & Kegan Paul, London, 1958), 32–33.

38 Professor Hoffmann, *Modern Magic* (Sterling Paperbacks, New Delhi, 1997), 271.

39 Whaley, B., *Encyclopedic Dictionary of Magic 1584–1988* (Jeff Busby Magic Inc., Oakland, CA, 1989), 195.

40 Ibid. 195.

41 Scot, Reginald, and Forrester, Reginald, *The Annotated Discovery of Witchcraft.* Privately printed, 2000.

42 Read, Bob, "The French Connection," *Magic* 6, no. 11, July 1997, 56–61.

43 Professor Hoffmann, op. cit., 272.

44 Maskelyne, Nevil, and Devant, David, *Our Magic* (Fleming Books, Berkeley Heights, NJ, 1946), 116.

45 Professor Hoffmann, op. cit., 272.

46 Sachs, Edwin T., *Sleight of Hand* (Magic Limited, Oakland, CA, 1979), 52.

47 Polanyi, Michael, *Personal Knowledge*, 50.

48 Maskelyne, Nevil, and Devant, David, op. cit., 102.

49 Polanyi, Michael, *Personal Knowledge*, 65.

50 Gelwick, Richard, op cit., 70.

51 Polanyi, Michael, *The Study of Man*, 31.

52 Polanyi, Michael, *The Tacit Dimension*, 17.

53 Hacking, Ian, *Representing and Intervening* (Cambridge University Press, Cambridge, 1983), 31.

54 Rouse, Joseph, "Understanding Scientific Practices," in Biagioli, Mario, ed., *The Science Studies Reader* (Routledge, New York, 1999), 450.

55 Ibid., 489.

56 Hacking, Ian, op. cit., 31.

57 Ibid., 54.

58 Ibid., 150.

59 Ibid., 185.

60 Gill, Jerry, *The Tacit Mode* (SUNY Press, New York, 2000), 8.

61 Hacking, Ian, op. cit., 131.

62 Ibid., 149.

63 Polanyi, Michael, *Personal Knowledge* (University of Chicago Press, Chicago, 1958), 49.

64 Ibid., 162.

65 Hacking, Ian, op. cit., 150.

66 Polanyi, Michael, op. cit., 88.

67 Ibid., 89.

68 Ibid., 50.

69 Hacking, Ian, op. cit., 189.

70 Ibid., 191.

71 Scott, Drusilla, *Everyman Revived* (Eerdmans Publishing Co, Grand Rapids, MI,1995), 115.

72 Polanyi, Michael, op. cit., 54.

73 Hacking, Ian, op. cit., 168.

74 Ibid., 167.

75 Ibid., 179.

76 Ibid., 180.

77 Ibid.

78 Shapin, Steven, and Schaffer, Simon, *Leviathan and the Air-Pump* (Princeton University Press, Princeton, NJ, 1985), 225.

79 Ibid., 225.

80 Ibid., 226.

81 Ibid., 229.

82 Ibid., 235.

83 Ibid., 230.

84 Polanyi, Michael, op. cit., 53.

85 Shapin, Steven, and Schaffer, Simon, op. cit., 281.

86 Ibid., 344.

87 Gill, Jerry, op. cit., 52.

88 Prosch, Harry, *Michael Polanyi: A Critical Exposition* (SUNY Press, New York, 1986), 111.

89 Gill, Jerry, op. cit., 53.

90 Polanyi, Michael, *The Tacit Dimension* (Anchor Books, New York, 1967), 25.

91 Polanyi, Michael, *Personal Knowledge*, 64.

92 Prosch, Harry, op. cit., 50.

93 Gill, Jerry, op. cit.,60.

94 Polanyi, Michael, *Personal Knowledge*, 300.

95 Grene, Marjorie, *A Philosophical Testament* (Open Court Publishing, Chicago, 1999), 18.

96 Gelwick, Richard, *The Way of Discovery* (Wipf and Stock Publishers, Eugene, OR, 1977), 150.

97 Polanyi, Michael, *Personal Knowledge*, vii.

98 Ibid., 65.

99 Polanyi, Michael, *Science, Faith and Society* (University of Chicago Press, Chicago, 1964), 50.

100 Hahn, Lewis, and Auxier, Randall, eds,, *The Philosophy of Marjorie Grene* (Open Court Publishing, Chicago, 2003), 58.

101 Gelwick, Richard, op. cit., 141.

102 Gill, Jerry, op. cit., 60.

103 Ibid., 67.

104 Epistemic humility is a notion that I came up with in 2000 when I began research for a paper I was writing called "Rational Mediation." It is, in short, the idea that we must remain open to other people's ideas and ways of seeing the world and that we must maintain a sense of humility when it comes to our knowledge and how we choose to use it, represent it and make decisions based on it. It's about being open. It's about being inclusive from a philosophical, theological and sociological perspective. None of us has a God's-eye view of the world, nor should we behave as if we do. Too many horrible things have been said, written and done in the name of having the key to absolute truth.

105 Gill, Jerry, *The Tacit Mode* (SUNY Press, New York, 2000), 196.

106 Gelwick, Richard, The Way of Discovery (Wipf and Stock Publishers, Eugene, OR, 1977), 65.

107 Ibid.

108 Polanyi, Michael, *Personal Knowledge* (University of Chicago Press, Chicago, 1958), 60.

109 Ibid., 404.

110 Einstein, Albert, tr. Lawson, Robert W., *Relativity: The Special and General Theory* (Random House, New York, 1961), 122–127.

111 Grene, Marjorie, *The Knower and the Known* (Faber, London, 1966), 146.

112 Scott, Drusilla, *Everyman Revived: The Common Sense of Michael Polanyi* (Eerdmans Publishing Company, Grand Rapids, MI, 1995), 97.

113 Aristotle, *Nicomachean Ethics*, in *Introduction to Aristotle*, McKeon, Richard, ed. (Random House, New York, 1947), 331, 337.

114 Polanyi, Michael, op. cit., 3.

115 Grene, Marjorie, *A Philosophical Testament* (Open Court Publishing, Chicago, 1995), 15.

BIBLIOGRAPHY

Anderson, Mary B. *Do No Harm.* Lynne Rienner Publishers, Boulder, Colorado, 1999.

Avery, Christopher. "Cruelty Charges at Humane Society." *The Globe and Mail*, November 27, 2011.

Barthes, Roland. *Camera Lucida.* Farrar, Straus & Giroux, New York, 1981.

Baudrillard, Jean. *Simulations.* Semiotext(e). Columbia University Press, New York, 1983.

Bernstein, Richard J. "Evil and the Temptation of Theodicy." Critchley, Simon, and Bernasconi, Robert. *The Cambridge Companion to Lévinas.* Cambridge University Press, New York, 2002.

Blake, William. "The Poison Tree." In Williams, O., ed. *Immortal Poems of the English Language.* Simon & Schuster, New York, 1952.

Buckingham, Geoffrey. *It's Easier Than You Think.* Magic Inc., Chicago, 1979.

Bukatman, Scott. *Blade Runner.* British Film Institute, London, 1997.

Chan, Victor. *The Wisdom of Forgiveness.* Riverhead Books, New York, 2004.

Chomsky, Noam. *Aspects of the Theory of Syntax.* The MIT Press, Cambridge, MA, 1965.

Clarke, David B., ed. *The Cinematic City.* Routledge, New York, 1997.

Collins, H. M. "The TEA Set." In Biaioli, M., ed. *The Science Studies Reader.* Routledge, New York, 1999.

Critchley, Simon, and Bernasconi, R., eds. *The Cambridge Companion to Lévinas.* Cambridge University Press, New York, 2002.

Curry, Paul. *Magician's Magic.* 1942. Dover Publications, Mineola, New York, 2003.

Dallaire, Romeo. *Shake Hands with the Devil.* Random House Canada, Toronto, 2003.

De Beauvoir, Simone. *The Ethics of Ambiguity.* Citadel Press, New York, 1976.

De Saint-Exupéry, Antoine. *The Little Prince.* Harvest Books, New York, 2001.

Descartes, René, tr. Cress, Donald A. *Discourse on Method.* Hackett Publishing, Indianapolis, IN, 1998.

Descartes, René, tr. Voss, Steven H. *The Passions of the Soul.* Hackett Publishing, Indianapolis, IN, 1989.

Dorter, K. "Philosopher-Rulers: How Contemplation Becomes Action." In *Ancient Philosophy 21* (2001).

Dostoyevsky, Fyodor, tr. Magarshack, D. *The Brothers Karamazov*. Penguin Books, London, 1958.

Dupré, Julie. *Skyscrapers*. Black Dog & Leventhal Publishers, New York, 2001.

Einstein, Albert, tr. Lawson, Robert W. *Relativity: The Special and the General Theory*. Random House, New York, 1961.

Foucault, Michel. *Discipline and Punish*. Vintage Books, New York, 1977.

Fowles, John. "Seeing Nature Whole." *Harper's Magazine*, November 1979.

Frede, D. "The Question of Being." In Guignon, C. B., ed. *The Cambridge Companion to Heidegger*. Cambridge University Press, New York, 1993.

Friedman, Milton. "The Social Responsibility of Business." *The New York Times Magazine*. September 13, 1970.

Gelwick, Richard. *The Way of Discovery: An Introduction to the Thought of Michael Polanyi*. Wipf and Stock Publishers, Eugene, OR, 1977.

Gill, Jerry. *The Tacit Mode: Michael Polanyi's Postmodern Philosophy*. SUNY Press, New York, 2000.

Grene, Marjorie G. *The Knower and the Known*. Faber, London, 1966.

———. "Tacit Knowing: Grounds for a Revolution in Philosophy." *Journal of the British Society for Phenomenology 8*, no. 3 (October 1977).

———. *A Philosophical Testament*. Open Court Publishing, Chicago, 1995.

———. "The Personal and the Subjective." *Tradition and Discovery 22* (1995–1996).

Hacking, Ian. *Representing and Intervening*. Cambridge University Press, Cambridge, 1983.

Hahn, Lewis E., and Auxier, Randall. *The Philosophy of Marjorie Grene*. Open Court Publishing, Chicago, 2003.

Hall, H. "Intentionality and World." In *The Cambridge Companion to Heidegger*, Guignon, C. B., ed. Cambridge University Press, New York, 1993.

Hammond, Nicholas, ed. *The Cambridge Companion to Pascal*. Cambridge University Press, Cambridge, 2003.

Heidegger, Martin. "Building Dwelling Thinking." In Krell, D. F., ed. *Martin Heidegger: Basic Writings*, Revised and Expanded Edition. HarperCollins, New York, 1993.

———. "The Origin of the Work of Art." In Krell, D. F., ed. *Martin Heidegger: Basic Writings*, Revised and Expanded Edition. HarperCollins, New York, 1993.

Hochschild, Adam. *Bury the Chains*. Mariner Books, New York, 2006.

———. *King Leopold's Ghost*. Mariner Books, New York, 1999.

Jopling, David. *Self-Knowledge and the Self*. Routledge, New York, 2000.

Kuhn, Annette, ed. *Alien Zone II*. Verso, New York, 1999.

Kane, Jeffrey. *Beyond Empiricism: Michael Polanyi Reconsidered*. Peter Lang Publishing, New York, 1984.

Khalfa, Jean. "Pascal's Theory of Knowledge." In Hammond, N., ed. *The Cambridge Companion to Pascal*. Cambridge University Press, Cambridge, 2003.

Kierkegaard, Søren, tr. Hong, H., and Hong, E. *Fear and Trembling; Repetition*. Princeton University Press, Princeton, NJ, 1983.

Kuhn, Thomas S. *The Structure of Scientific Revolutions*. Chicago University Press, Chicago, 1967.

Lévinas, Emmanuel. *Totality and Infinity*. Duquesne University Press, Pittsburgh, PA, 1969.

———. *Ethics and Infinity*. Duquesne University Press, Pittsburgh, PA, 1982.

McKeon, Richard, ed. *Introduction to Aristotle*. Random House, New York, 1947.

Macquarrie, John. *Martin Heidegger*. John Knox Press, Louisville, KY, 1968.

Maskelyne, Nevil, and Devant, D. *Our Magic*. Fleming Books, Berkeley Heights, NJ, 1946.

Merleau-Ponty, Maurice. *Phenomenology of Perception*. Routledge & Kegan Paul, London, 1962.

Niebuhr, Reinhold. *The Irony of American History*. University of Chicago Press, Chicago, 2008.

Plato, tr. West, Thomas G., and West, Grace Starry. *Texts on Socrates—The Apology*. Cornell University Press, New York, 1984.

Polanyi, Michael. *Personal Knowledge*. University of Chicago Press, Chicago, 1958.

———. *The Study of Man*. Routledge & Kegan Paul, London, 1958.

———. *Science, Faith and Society*. University of Chicago Press, Chicago, 1964.

———. *The Tacit Dimension*. Anchor Books, New York, 1967.

———. *Knowing and Being: Essays*. Grene, Marjorie, ed. University of Chicago Press, Chicago, 1969.

Polanyi, Michael, and Prosch, Harry. *Meaning*. University of Chicago Press, Chicago, 1975.

Popper, Karl R. "Epistemology Without a Knowing Subject." In Popper, Karl R. *Objective Knowledge: An Evolutionary Approach*. Clarendon Press, Oxford, 1973.

Professor Hoffman. *Modern Magic*. Sterling Paperbacks, New Delhi, 1997.

Prosch, Harry. *Michael Polanyi: A Critical Exposition*. SUNY Press, Albany, NY, 1986.

Read, B. "The French Connection." *Magic* 6 (1997).

Rogers, B. "Pascal's Life and Times." Hammond, Nicholas, ed. *The Cambridge Companion to Pascal*. Cambridge University Press, Cambridge, 2003.

Roth, David. *Expert Coin Magic*. D. Robbins & Co., Cranbury, NJ, 1985.

Rouse, J. "Understanding Scientific Practices." In Biagoli, M., ed. *The Science Studies Reader*. Routledge, New York, 1999.

Roychoudhuri, Onnesha. "The End of Poverty: An Interview with Jeffrey Sachs"

<www.motherjones.com/news/qa/2005/05/jeffrey_sachs.html>.

Rucyahana, John. *The Bishop of Rwanda*. Thomas Nelson, Nashville, TN, 2007.

Russon, John. *Human Experience: Philosophy, Neurosis, and the Elements of Everyday Life*. SUNY Press, New York, 2003.

Ryan, Michael, and Kellner, Douglas, eds. *Camera Politica*. Indiana University Press, Indianapolis, 1988.

Ryle, Gilbert. *Collected Papers, Volume Two*. Hutchinson, London, 1971.

Sachs, Edwin T. *Sleight of Hand*. Magic Limited, Oakland, CA, 1979.

Sachs, Jeffrey. *The End of Poverty*. Penguin Press, New York, 2005.

Sacks, Oliver. *The Man Who Mistook His Wife for a Hat*. HarperCollins, New York, 1970.

Sayer, Karen, and Moore, John. *Science Fiction: Critical Frontiers*. St. Martin's Press, New York, 2000.

Schumpeter, Joseph A. *The Process of Creative Destruction*. Edward Elgar Publishing, 1942.

Scot, Reginald, and Forrester, Reginald. *The Annotated Discovery of Witchcraft*. Privately printed, 2000.

Scott, Drusilla. *Everyman Revived: The Common Sense of Michael Polanyi*. Erdmans Publishing, Grand Rapids, MI, 1995.

Shapin, Steven. "The House of Experiment in Seventeenth-Century England." In Biagoli, M., ed. *The Science Studies Reader*. Routledge, New York, 1999.

Shapin, Steven, and Schaffer, Simon. *Leviathan and the Air-Pump: Hobbes, Boyle, and the Experimental Life*. Princeton University Press, Princeton, NJ, 1985.

Sibum, H. O. "Reworking the Mechanical Value of Heat." *Studies in the History and Philosophy of Science 26* (1995).

Smillie, Ian. *Patronage or Parntership*. Kumarian Press, Bloomfield, 2001.

Snyder, F. W., and Pronko, N. H. *Vision Without Spatial Inversion*. University of Wichita Press, Wichita, KS, 1952.

Stratton, G. M. "Vision Without Inversion of the Retinal Image." *Psychological Review 4* (1897).

Talbot, John. *Grounds for Agreement*. Rowman & Littlefield, Oxford, 2004.

Tannen, Louis. *Stars of Magic*. Louis Tannen Inc., New York, 1975.

Taylor, C. "Merleau-Ponty and the Epistemological Picture." Carman, T., and Hansen, M. B. N., eds. *The Cambridge Companion to Merleau-Ponty*. Cambridge University Press, Cambridge, 2003.

Tutu, Desmond. *No Future Without Forgiveness*. Image Books, New York, 2000.

Ung, Loung. *First They Killed My Father: A Daughter of Cambodia Remembers*. HarperCollins, New York, 2000.

Wakefield, Neville. *Postmodernism: The Twilight of the Real*. Pluto Press, London, 1990.

Whaley, B. *Encyclopedic Dictionary of Magic, 1584–1988*. Jeff Busby Magic, Oakland, CA,1989.

Wiesenthal, Simon. *The Sunflower*. Schocken Books, New York, 1997.

Wilde, Oscar. "The Ballad of Reading Jail." *The Collected Works of Oscar Wilde*. Wordsworth Editions, Hertfordshire, UK, 1997.

Wilson, Johanthan. "Vision That Grips You." *Leadership by Soul Newsletter*, January 2011.

Witmer, A. E. "Tacit Knowing, Truthful Knowing: The Life and Thought of Michael Polanyi." Audio recording by Mars Hill Audio. Berea Publications, Charlottesville, PA, 1999.

www.ingramcontent.com/pod-product-compliance
Lightning Source LLC
Chambersburg PA
CBHW070805270326
41927CB00010B/2307